Advance praise for *Without Apology*:

"Here is one of the greatest English-language theologians of our time doing what great theologians do—directing and focusing a huge range of sophisticated scholarship and reflection into life-giving communication for the gathering of believers. Every bit as unfailingly fresh, rich and nourishing as the rest of his work."

—Rowan Williams
104th Archbishop of Canterbury and
Master, Magdalene College at
Cambridge University

"Stanley Hauerwas is virtually unique today in his dual identity as a major systematic theologian who is also deeply committed to the day-in, day-out preaching vocation. Like Karl Barth before him, Hauerwas believes there is no point in systematic theology except to tell the preachers what to preach. . . . What a gift to the church, and to other preachers in particular! Here is a model found almost nowhere else today: in his own pungent and irresistible idiom, Hauerwas illustrates why the church under pressure must have the systematic theologian in order to understand and affirm what it believes, and why the systematic theologian must be a preacher in order to test and validate what he teaches. Lay people, you will relish this banquet—and preachers, you can study at the feet of a master."

—Fleming Rutledge
author of *Not Ashamed of the Gospel* and
The Undoing of Death

"If you have joyfully followed Hauerwas the radically faithful, unapologetic theologian over the years, you will love listening to Hauerwas the preacher. And if you have read Stanley's theological writing and have found it difficult, you will really love these sermons. Here is Hauerwas testifying to the church, clearly, joyfully restoring the adventure of being Christian. Stanley's wonderment at the riches of Christian believing, his ability to engage in deep intellectual work in a playful way, as well as his marvelous subservience to Christian truth make these sermons unforgettable. With Stanley loose in the pulpit, daring to say what God puts on his mind, and a compromised, struggling, sometimes faithful, often foolish church before him, be prepared for fireworks. Wonderful!"

—Will Willimon
Bishop of the United Methodist Church (ret.)
and Professor of the Practice of Christian Ministry,
Duke University

"What is holiness? How does baptism change our experience of this world? Why are so many in ministry sexually irresponsible? Here Hauerwas offers what many Christians long for and never find: practical reflection on what it is to live and think as a Christian. These sermons draw upon deep learning and critical appraisal of the theological tradition, yet they speak plainly to anyone who goes to church and sometimes wonders why, to us who hear the words of Scripture and repeat the creeds, often wondering how to mean what we say."

—Ellen F. Davis
Amos Ragan Kearns Distinguished Professor
of Bible and Practical Theology
Duke Divinity School

WITHOUT APOLOGY

Sermons for Christ's Church

WITHOUT Sermons for Christ's Church
APOLOGY

STANLEY HAUERWAS

Seabury Books
NEW YORK

Unless otherwise noted, the Scripture quotations contained herein are from the New Revised Standard Version Bible, copyright © 1989 by the Division of Christian Educa-tion of the National Council of Churches of Christ in the U.S.A. Used by permission. All rights reserved.

Library of Congress Cataloging-in-Publication Data

Hauerwas, Stanley, 1940-
 Without apology : sermons for Christ's church / Stanley Hauerwas.
    p. cm.
 Includes bibliographical references.
 ISBN 978-1-59627-248-4 (pbk.) -- ISBN 978-1-59627-249-1 (ebook) 1. Hauerwas, Stanley, 1940---Sermons. 2. Sermons, American. I. Title.
 BX4827.H34A5 2013
 252--dc23

                         2013011557

Cover painting, *Incarnate—Be With Us Now*, by Roger Hutchison
(www.rogerpaintings.com)
Cover design by Laurie Klein Westhafer
Typeset by Rose Design

Seabury Books
19 East 34th Street
New York, New York 10016

www.churchpublishing.org

An imprint of Church Publishing Incorporated

Printed in the United States of America

Contents

PART III

Diverse Occasions

PART IV

Sermons on the Priesthood

PART V

Other Writings

Preface

I am often asked, "How many books have you written?" My truthful answer must be, "I have no idea." There is a list of books that bear my name on my CV so I guess I could count them, but I have no interest in doing so. I am not sure why I resist knowing how many books I have published, but I think I resist quantification because the books are only means to an end for me. What I care about is how some reader may find this sermon, or that sentence or chapter, in a book helpful for their life as a Christian.

I think I also resist quantifying my work because I do not like what the possessive "my" seems to suggest. What I write, and this is particularly true of sermons, is so dependent on the help of others I have difficulty locating the "my." I owe a particular debt, for example, to Carole Baker, my long-time assistant, for the "work-over" she gives these sermons. Paula Gilbert, my long-time wife, often makes suggestions not only about what I say but how I might say what I say. Paula is an eloquent preacher, celebrant, and human being and I hope these sermons, in some small measure, reflect her wisdom and grace.

Paula and I—as staff member and layperson, respectively—have now been at the Church of the Holy Family in Chapel Hill, North Carolina, for over ten years. I do not think we could make sense of our lives without Holy Family. Holy Family is an

Episcopal Church which means we are indebted to The Episcopal Church. It, therefore, gives me great satisfaction that *Without Apology* is published by Church Publishing and bears the imprint of Seabury Books. I hope this book might be received as a gesture of gratitude for the existence of The Episcopal Church—even with all of its confusions. At the very least this book is my way to say "thank you" for the hospitality that has been extended to us.

In particular I am indebted to Father Clarke French, the rector of Holy Family, for entrusting me to preach at Holy Family. He is an extraordinary priest and good friend. I am equally beholden to Father Timothy Kimbrough, the former rector of Holy Family and now Dean of Christ Church Cathedral in Nashville, for suggesting to Bishop Bauerschmidt that I be made canon theologian of the Cathedral. I am deeply grateful to the congregations of Holy Family and Christ Church for their willingness to have me become part of their life.

Introduction

Why Another Book of Sermons?

"What are you working on now?" is the standard question academics ask one another after they have exchanged pleasantries. The question seems innocent, but it is often intended to discover if the one questioned has "dried up," that is, whether they have pretty much said what they have to say. I do not know if I have said all that I have to say, but since what I have to say is not mine to say but God's, all I know is I have to keep at it. It turns out that sermons are, for me, crucial for thinking about what needs to be said.

I am also often asked, "What are your plans for retirement?" I never know what to say other than to observe that I have never lived my life or done my work according to any plan. I have always done what people asked me to do, and I assume I will continue to do what I am asked to do in retirement. In particular, I hope I will be asked to preach.

I am a layperson. I regard it a great gift to be asked to preach. I am usually asked to preach well in advance, which means I have some time to think about the appointed scripture as well as where we are in the church year. I am sure I spend as much time thinking about and writing a sermon as I do on my so-called "scholarly" work. I have nothing but admiration for those who preach on a weekly basis and who do not have the time I am given to prepare and write. At least one of the reasons I make these sermons available is not only to honor those who preach on a more regular basis, but also in the hope that they might find what I do some use for what they do.

Without Apology: Sermons for Christ's Church is the fourth book of sermons I have published. Actually, it is my fifth book of sermons if you count, as I would like, *Cross-Shattered Christ: Meditations on the Seven Last Words of Jesus*.[1] I continue to give and publish sermons because, as I wrote in the Introduction to *A Cross-Shattered Church: Reclaiming the Theological Heart of Preaching*, the demands intrinsic to the task of preaching force me to think thoughts and make associations I would not otherwise make. I find preaching to be theologically the most fertile work I do.

I hesitate, however, to contrast preaching and academic theology. I have no desire to give aid and comfort to the anti-intellectualism that possesses so many in the ministry today. The arid character of much of academic theology is regrettable to be sure, but I know my more academic work is necessary for helping

---

1. Previous books of sermons are *Unleashing the Scripture: Freeing the Bible from Captivity to America* (Nashville: Abingdon Press, 1993); *Disrupting Time: Sermons, Prayers, and Sundries* (Eugene, OR: Cascade Books, 2004); *A Cross-Shattered Church: Reclaiming the Theological Heart of Preaching* (Grand Rapids: Brazos Press, 2009); and *Working with Words: On Learning to Speak Christian* (Eugene, OR: Cascade Books, 2011). I hesitate to include *Cross-Shattered Christ: Meditations on the Seven Last Words* (Grand Rapids: Brazos Press, 2004) because it is not a collection but, as the title suggests, meditations on Jesus' last words. It is, however, a book of sermons delivered at St. Thomas Fifth Avenue during Holy Week. Nor is *Unleashing the Scripture* strictly understood a collection of sermons, even though the second half of the book consists in what I call "sermonic exhibits." Though often criticized for not attending sufficiently to scripture, I use the sermons in *Unleashing the Scripture*, as well as the other books of sermons, to exemplify the argument I make in *Unleashing the Scripture* for why the historical-critical method cannot and should not determine *the* meaning of the text.

me preach and my preaching informs what is usually regarded as my more "scholarly" work. As far as I am concerned I can discern no difference in the work I do as an academic theologian and when I am writing a sermon. I hope that is true for the sermons that comprise *Without Apology*.

Another reason I continue to publish my sermons is I so value the readership they make possible. Theology is a church discipline, but most theologians are paid to do their work by universities. There are some real benefits to this arrangement. At least by their location in universities, in principle theologians can learn from as well as engage the work of their more secular colleagues. But the disadvantage is theology is now written and read primarily by other theologians. I have never wanted to so restrict my work. I regard it a great gift that theologians should have a readership not limited to other academics. The people who comprise that readership are called Christians. I should like to think that these sermons are written for that constituency within and without the university.

I cannot pretend that the sermons in *Without Apology* represent any striking new development in my work. I remain committed to helping us recover our ability to speak Christian without apology.[2] I suspect some might justifiably think *Without Apology* could have been used to entitle almost any book I have written. There is some truth to that, but at least one of the reasons I persist in publishing my sermons is to show that what William Placher characterized as "unapologetic theology" can be preached.[3] Indeed, I hope my sermons serve to call into question the presumption that

---

2. For what it might mean "to speak Christian," see my *Working with Words*.

3. William Placher, *Unapologetic Theology: A Christian Voice in a Pluralistic Conversation* (Louisville: Westminster John Knox, 1989).

I have no interest in apologetics. Rather, I should like to think that how I preach exemplifies Karl Barth's contention that a "respectable dogmatics could be good apologetics."[4]

Why, therefore, have I titled this book *Without Apology*? One reason is to contrast my understanding of the task of preaching with that of Paul Tillich in his collection of sermons titled *The Shaking of the Foundations*.[5] In the Preface to *The Shaking of the Foundations*, Tillich observed that given the development of modernity "a sermon in traditional Biblical terms would have no meaning" for the congregations associated with universities before whom he preached. Accordingly, Tillich says he "was obliged to seek a language which expresses in other terms the human experience to which the Biblical and ecclesiastical terminology point." Tillich characterized his "method" as an exercise in apologetics.[6]

To be obliged to seek a language which expresses in "other terms" the "human experience" to which the biblical and ecclesial terminology points seems innocent enough, but from my perspective that is to give away the store. Why does Tillich assume that there is something called "human experience" that must find expression in a language? To so understand language reproduces the mistaken view that language is one thing and human experience another thing. That is why Tillich assumes that the "Biblical and ecclesial terminological points"—what,

---

4. Karl Barth, *The Humanity of God* (Richmond: John Knox Press, 1963), 20.

5. Paul Tillich, *The Shaking of the Foundations* (New York: Scribner's Sons, 1948).

6. Tillich, "Preface" in *The Shaking of the Foundations*. In the "Introduction" to Will Willimon's and my book, *Preaching to Strangers* (Louisville, KY: Westminster John Knox, 1992), I called attention as well as criticized Tillich's understanding of apologetics. I love *Preaching to Strangers* but it is a book that few have read, which is why I think it worthwhile to engage Tillich yet again.

after all, is a "terminological point"?—can be translated into another language without loss.

I call attention to Tillich's position because I think he represents a widespread understanding of the challenge that must be met by anyone who would take up the task of preaching. It is assumed, interestingly enough by those who are often self-identified as theologically conservative as well as those who think of themselves as liberals, that those to whom they preach must find what is said in the sermon to be intelligible or relevant without challenging the hearer's "experience." From such a perspective a good sermon is thought to be one in which some "meaning" can be derived from what has been said that confirms what I thought prior to hearing the sermon.

In contrast I simply do not speculate about what "modern people" can or should be able to hear or believe. I am, or at least I should like to think I am, a modern person who is relatively well educated. But I have no idea how being modern may or may not inhibit my ability to be a Christian. I suspect my ability, or lack thereof, to be a Christian has less to do with being modern than it does with the everyday challenge of being a human being. I have no reason to deny that the task of being human may have peculiar and distinct form in our time, but when all is said and done it is about birth and death and all that comes between those two realities. To be sure, as some of these sermons suggest, it is extremely important to understand the way birth and death are shaped by our "modern" presumptions.

My strong identification with Karl Barth and John Howard Yoder, whose work informs the Christological center of my work, and the emphasis on the church may have given some the impression that the way I do theology has little to say about what it means to be human. Though it is certainly true that I am a sworn enemy of pietistic accounts of the faith, that is, the presumption that being Christian is just another way to say it is all about us, I should like to think that I have had and continue to have something to say about the difficulty of being human.[7] Indeed I would be quite satisfied if some might view my theology as a form of Christian humanism. In particular it is my hope that these sermons display compelling insights for Christian and non-Christian alike about how we must live if we are to flourish as creatures created in God's image.

Insight, or perhaps more accurately, wisdom, I take to be the heart of the matter. A "respectable dogmatics" is good apologetics just to the extent it can be shown that the illumination of our lives by the Gospel is inseparable from the theological concepts and convictions that make the insights possible.[8] That is why good preaching is, in Sam Wells's language, a matter of "speaking the truth."[9] Wells acknowledges that truth is an ambivalent word, but that is why it is so important that we use it. Truth on

---

7. I hope to have ready before long a collection of essays that deal with the difficulty of being human that might serve as a companion book to *Without Apology*.

8. David Hart rightly suggests that "every true historical revolution is a conceptual revolution first and the magnitude of any large revision of the conditions or premises of human life (to say nothing of the time required for it to bear historical fruit) is determined by the magnitude of the prior 'spiritual' achievement. Considered thus, the rise of Christianity was surely an upheaval of unprecedented and still unequaled immensity." *Atheist Delusions: The Christian Revolution and Its Fashionable Enemies* (New Haven: Yale University Press, 2009), 175. I think no one does this better than Herbert McCabe. For example, he begins a sermon on Mark 10:17–22 with the comment, "I thought we might reflect a minute or two on the connection Jesus makes between possessions and sorrow." You cannot help but rightly be drawn into his thick account of how possessions make us "takers" unable to enjoy the giftedness of being. In *God, Christ, and Us*, ed. Brian Davies (London: Continuum, 2003), 53–57.

9. Samuel Wells, *Speaking the Truth: Preaching in a Pluralistic Culture* (Nashville: Abingdon, 2008).

the one hand means "an ingenuous, candid, thoughtful interjection of sometimes uncomfortable, disruptive, and disconcerting but nonetheless life-giving wisdom" but, on the other hand, "when spoken within the church, *truth* means Christ, the image of the invisible God."[10]

To speak the truth, according to Wells, means perceiving how the transformation accomplished in Christ has permeated and overturned every detail of human existence. To speak the truth does not require translation but rather a confidence that what we say when we say God was in Christ makes a difference for how our lives and the world is rightly understood. Preaching is the gift God has given the church so that our lives can be located within God's life by having our existence storied by the Gospel.

"To speak the truth" may suggest that if sermons are to be faithful to the Gospel they must be very serious, if not ponderous. Yet the sermons Wells provides to exemplify what speaking the truth looks like in *To Speak the Truth* are anything but ponderous. Indeed, he often employs humor not in an attempt to "lighten" what he has to say, but rather because the humor is intrinsic to the argument he is making. God's great joke on the world is surely that out of all the peoples of the world God chose Israel to be the promised people. Who, moreover, could have anticipated the resurrection? This is a God of surprise and surprise is at the heart of humor. So to speak the truth must be done, as Wells does so well, with an infectious joy that reflects our faith in a God that does not need our protection.

Not only must preachers risk being funny from time to time, but they must also, if Wells is to be imitated, be willing to be entertaining. For it is surely one of the tasks of preaching

---

10. Ibid., ix.

to free us from our self-absorption by offering a compelling vision of the world Christ's cross has made real. So I hope readers of these sermons will find themselves from time to time laughing at something I have said, as well as being entertained by the way I approach a text. For example, the snide remarks I make about Episcopalians not coming to church to be touched in "Tenderness" I think is not only funny but true. The response I received to that sermon certainly confirmed that characterization of my Episcopal brothers and sisters.

Another way to put these matters is that rather than trying to translate the Gospel into a different but allegedly more accessible language, I seek to help us learn again the odd grammar of Christian speech and how that grammar helps us see the sheer contingency of our existence. Ivan Illich observes that the contingent character of our existence means we must learn again and again that we live in a world that does not carry within itself the reason for its own existence. Illich maintains, "The cat over there as well as four red roses which bloomed during the night, is a gift. It is a gift from that Creator who keeps beings in existence and, by understanding things in this way, we can also see our own activity in an entirely new light."[11] From such a perspective, preaching is the ongoing exercise that allows the Gospel to shed light on the oddness of the everyday.

I used a word to characterize the sermons of Sam Wells that is seldom employed to describe the work done in sermons. I suggested his sermons are "arguments." I should like to think that the sermons in *Without Apology* are also arguments. They are arguments because I often try to counter presumptions that

---

11. Ivan Illich, *The Rivers North of the Future: The Testament of Ivan Illich*, as told to David Cayley (Toronto: Anansi Press, 2005), 65–66.

domesticate the Gospel or make it difficult to live as a Christian. One of the ways I do that is by characterizing as well as I can a position or reaction to the text that I think impedes our understanding of the Gospel. I do not call attention in the sermon itself to the argument as an argument, but I certainly understand my task to be an attempt to argue against what I can only characterize as the sentimentalities of our age that are too often identified as Christian.

That means I often try to characterize as sympathetically as I can the position against which I am trying to mount an argument. For example, my use of Foucault's account of the modern prison in "Prisoners No More" I think proved to be a very effective way to make candid our attitude toward the antitheses in the Sermon on the Mount. Behind the rhetorical strategy of that sermon is my judgment that one of the characteristics of our lives is a terrible loneliness. To suggest how the Sermon on the Mount can provide an alternative to such loneliness I think truthfully helps us see that Jesus really is the alternative to such loneliness.

That I think of these sermons as arguments entails a very definite politics concerning the place of the church in the world. That I put the matter in terms of the dualism between church/world is itself an indication of the politics that shape these sermons. The dualism between church and world does not assume that the Gospel is one thing and politics another. That is why I do not understand my task to be convincing allegedly apolitical congregations that they ought as faithful Christians to be involved in politics. I am not, of course, opposed to Christians taking political positions as Christians, but I try to help us see that the Gospel does not *have* political implications because the Gospel *is* a politics.

"The Gospel is a politics" is a play on the title of John Howard Yoder's great book *The Politics of Jesus: Vicit Agnus Noster*.[12]
It is my hope that these sermons challenge the presumption that
Yoder's understanding of the church's mission to embody mate-
rially the "politics of Jesus" does not require a withdrawal from
the world. Rather, by being the church, the world is provided
with alternatives that are otherwise unavailable. In fact, I understand preaching as the exercise and exemplification of a truthful
political authority that the world desperately needs.

Yoder's position is often alleged to be so "radical" that there
is, in fact, no church that does or can exemplify his understanding of "the politics of Jesus." Critics ask: "Where is the church
that Yoder envisages?" I answer: "Where sermons are preached
without apology." I certainly think to so preach presumes that
we are living at the end of Christendom. We live in a time when
the church is losing its social and political power and this provides a rich opportunity for the recovery of the significance of
preaching. At the very least, in such a time those who gather
Sunday after Sunday to sit under the authority of the Word must
have some sense that being a Christian makes one different. I
try throughout these sermons to make articulate the challenges
Christians face as they negotiate the world, a world that ambigu-
ously represents a Christian past and a yet unknown future,
which can tempt us to miss the Christian difference.

The politics represented in these sermons is one of the reasons I have used the title *Without Apology: Sermons for Christ's
Church*. Apologetic theology, I fear too often, is a theology that
presumes an established church whose task it is to reinforce the

---

12. John Howard Yoder, *The Politics of Jesus: Vicit Agnus Noster* (Grand Rapids: Eerdmans, 1995).

presumptions of the established order. In such a world apologetics is the attempt to show that the way things are is the way things have to be. In contrast, I assume that the task of preaching is to show that the way things are is not the way things have to be. When done well, and I do not pretend to think I always do it well, to show the Gospel alternative to the way things are turns out to be a compelling apologetic.

Why I Do Not Explain

In the Introduction to my commentary on the Gospel of Matthew, I call attention to certain rules I tried to follow as I wrote that commentary. For example, I resolved to make no reference to the "Synoptic Problem." That I made no reference to the "Synoptic Problem" was one implication of my attempt to refrain from trying to get "behind" the text by employing the historical-critical method. In a similar fashion I tried to avoid all consciousness words because such words tempt us to use expressions such as: "What Matthew must have been thinking when he wrote X or Y is. . . ." My attempt to avoid consciousness words not only reflects my worries about certain philosophies of the mind that turn on notions of awareness, but it also reflects my commitment to avoid explaining the texts by getting behind them in order to show what they "really" must have meant.[13]

I call attention to the rules I tried to follow when I wrote the commentary on Matthew because I also follow those rules when I write sermons. So the reader will not find any reference to scholarship that shows us what the text really must have meant in its

---

13. Stanley Hauerwas, *Matthew: Brazos Theological Commentary on the Bible* (Grand Rapids: Brazos Press, 2006), 18–21.

"original" setting. I do read commentaries and monographs written by scripture scholars who often are primarily interested in the historical reconstruction of the text. I do so because I often find that they help me focus on a phrase or an aside that I am tempted to ignore. Historical work on scripture can be a gift to those of us not so trained as it prompts us to stop before words or phrases we are tempted to overlook as having no importance. Even those whose interests are primarily historical often make comments on the texts that are quite powerful. That they do so is not the result of their historical scholarship but rather it is a reflection of a profound humanity. That said, it nonetheless remains the case that the reading I do in the scholarly literature dealing with the assigned texts seldom shapes the sermon I write.[14]

A summarization of these rules can be found in the admonition "never explain." If you begin with the presumption that the texts of scripture are obscure because they are historically dated, e.g., they are irredeemably sexist, you will subject the text to a narrative that subordinates the text to an external standard that is not scriptural. I once suggested that one of the reasons Will Willimon is such an accomplished preacher is that he never explains. He never explains because he does not think the scripture needs to be rescued from that utopian place called the "original setting." In contrast, Willimon understands his task is to

---

14. For a powerful argument that the critical study of the scripture should not be made normative for how scripture is read, see Peter van Inwagen's chapter titled "Critical Studies of the New Testament" in his book *God, Knowledge and Mystery: Essays in Philosophical Theology* (Ithaca: Cornell University Press, 1995), 161–190. I confess I cannot help but take perverse delight in van Inwagen's summary declaration coming after close argument that he sees "that there is no reason for me to think that Critical Studies have established that the New Testament narratives are historically unreliable. In fact, there is no reason for me to think that they have established *any* important thesis about the New Testament" (189).

show how the scripture narrates us so that we are freed from the temptation to think it our task to try and resurrect some meaning from what is essentially a dead text.[15]

In my sermons I often try to anticipate how I, as well as those to whom I am preaching, am tempted to explain scripture in a manner that makes the explanation more determinative than the text itself. For example, in the sermon "Letting Go" I challenge the presumption that faith when compared to a mustard seed underwrites widespread subjective assumptions about what it means to "have faith." Accordingly, I suggest, given Paul's invitation to Timothy to join him "in suffering for the gospel" (2 Timothy 1:8), faith is best understood as a form of discipleship. In particular, to have faith is to learn to live out of control, which means we discover with Paul that to follow Jesus does not mean everything is going to come out all right.

Indeed, I should hope that one of the distinctive aspects of these sermons is the refusal to make them about us. Rather, I try never to forget that the subject of any sermon is the Triune God. We, of course, have a role by God's good grace in God's very life. But we do not get to determine God's relation to us; God has determined his relationship to us by becoming one of us. That contingency, that is, that God became a particular person named Jesus, makes it possible for us to live joyfully as contingent beings. Thus my attempt in "Facing Nothingness— Facing God" to confront what is often taken to be the unavoidable implications of evolution by showing how God's charge

---

15. For my essay "Explaining Why Will Willimon Never Explains," see *Disrupting Time: Sermons, Prayers, and Sundries* (Eugene, OR: Cascade, 2004), 224–33. I think it no accident that Willimon is a close student of Barth's preaching. See his *Conversations with Barth on Preaching* (Nashville: Abingdon Press, 2006).

to Isaiah reminds Israel—and us—that we are like grass that withers, that we are all in the care of God.

I should like to think that one of the most important characteristics of my preaching is the avoidance of sentimental appeals to "common experience." As soon as a preacher begins a sermon with "I cannot believe what my seven-year-old daughter recently said," you can quit listening. The subject of the sermon, no matter what else is said, will not direct attention to the witness of the scriptures to God. Rather the message of the sermon will be some form of romanticizing the child or family. Such a move is based on the presumption that it is our "common experience" that illumines the Gospel when in fact it should be the other way around. That is, the Gospel should illumine our relations, whether with our spouse, child, or friend, so that we may see more clearly how our tendency to romanticize these relations is more often than not an attempt to control them.

One criticism, and I certainly would not want to limit anyone reading these sermons to one criticism, is that I almost never use examples from the popular media. No doubt one of the reasons I make few references to popular culture is due to my lack of knowledge about popular culture. Age makes a difference and I am old. I simply cannot keep up with who is who and what is "in." I have never seen *American Idol* and I do not feel at a loss. I do not deny that there is a job for someone to provide a theological response to popular culture through preaching. I just do not understand that to be my job.

It may well be, moreover, that my lack of interest in much of what passes as popular culture reflects a class bias. But if that is the case I see no reason to apologize for having such a bias. I try very hard, however, to preach in a manner that people of diverse educational and class backgrounds can appreciate. Accordingly, these sermons, just as my books, have been written (and hopefully can be read) at several levels. If you have ears to hear or eyes to read, you may well know when I am making a critique of some philosophical or theological position without naming names. I cannot pretend my attempt to work at different levels is always successful, but I am determined to think people of diverse backgrounds can hear and/or read these sermons and think there is something in them that is worth thinking about.

It would never occur to me that I should try to "dumb down" a sermon. God has given us what is necessary for the Gospel to be understood by any congregation. The name of that gift is the Holy Spirit who enlivens the words we use. I am convinced nothing is more important for the recovery of preaching as a central act of the church than that those who preach trust that God is going to show up when the Word is rightly proclaimed. Too often those who preach fear those to whom they preach when in fact we ought to fear God. If God is rightly expected to show up, if God is rightly feared, then those who preach and those who hear will understand no explanation is required.

I have no idea if these reflections about how I try to avoid "explanation" amount to anything so grand as a theory of preaching. I have no ambition to become a subject in homiletics classes. In general I distrust most theories, but I think it important to try to be articulate about how and why I approach sermons in the way I do. I could say more about my method, such as why I try to first see what relation there might be between the texts assigned for the day, but I prefer to let the sermons speak for themselves. I hope I have said enough to make evaluations by others possible, evaluations about how these sermons and other's sermons help the church recover the gift we have been given in preaching God's good news.

Sermons for Christ's Church

The subtitle of this book may be too clever by half but I like it. Some of these sermons were delivered at Christ Church Cathedral in Nashville, Tennessee, but all these sermons presuppose that the church that makes preaching possible is "Christ's Church." By the latter designation I mean that the way I preach assumes that the people to whom I preach, whether they know it or not, belong to Christ. Put differently, I preach in a manner that tries to avoid privileging unbelief. I, of course, try to identify as well as criticize ways we who constitute Christ's body are unfaithful, but that is to presume we are Christ's church.

It is my good fortune to have been made the canon theologian at Christ Church Cathedral in Nashville, Tennessee. There is no great mystery about how this happened. Timothy Kimbrough, the former rector of the Church of the Holy Family, became the dean at Christ Church Cathedral in 2009. He asked me to preach on several occasions as well as conduct some adult forums. The Cathedral Chapter of Christ Church, with the approval of Bishop Bauerschmidt, asked me to become their canon theologian. I was honored to accept.

I confess I am not sure what it means to be a canon theologian, but I stand ready to perform the duties of that office. I assume that means doing what Dean Kimbrough and Bishop Bauerschmidt ask me to do. To be a canon theologian I am sure will be the highest ecclesial rank I will ever attain. When I was commissioned by Bishop Bauerschmidt I received the seal of the Cathedral "as a sign of the ministry that is entrusted to you under my direction and that of Dean Kimbrough." I take that ordering very seriously because it makes clear that my office as a theologian is one that is first and foremost of service to the bishop. I assume, therefore, that one of my responsibilities is to aid the bishop in his task of maintaining faithfulness to the tradition and unity between the churches under his care.

At least one of my responsibilities is to preach at Christ Church twice a year. To be asked to preach at Christ Church is a great privilege. I am not sure, but I suspect that the sermons I preach at the Church of the Holy Family have a more "personal" touch than those at Christ Church. I think that is why I have put the sermons I delivered at Holy Family before those at Christ Church. After all, the Church of the Holy Family in Chapel Hill, North Carolina, is my home parish. I assume a familiarity with the congregation at Holy Family that the other sermons in *Without Apology* cannot and do not have.

I have not tried to organize the sermons by category or theme. Rather I have simply grouped the sermons by where they were preached and in the order they were given. I do so partly to make clear that the sermons were never intended to build on one another. Each is meant to stand on its own feet. Nor do I think it would be useful for me to explain what I was trying to do in each sermon. If you need to explain what you were trying to do, then the sermon needs to be rewritten.

Though there is no necessary order to the sermons, I am quite happy that "Incarnation" is the opening sermon for the book. "Incarnation" clearly presumes that if we are to be more nearly faithful Christians we are going to return to the basics. The Christian people are dying for substantive articulations of the faith. To have a sermon like "Incarnation" connect the story of Jesus staying behind in Jerusalem with the doctrine of the Incarnation I think is crucial for a church that must learn to live after Christendom.

Also apparent in this sermon, which I hope is characteristic of a number of the sermons in this book, is how I connect "high doctrine," e.g., the doctrine of the Incarnation, with a concrete practice of the faith. That is why I call attention at the end of the sermon to the connection between the doctrine of the Incarnation and our reception of the body and blood of Christ at the Eucharist. Given our contemporary context I think it very important to help the Christian people recover the connections between what we do and why we do it.

I suspect some may wonder why I do not use sermons to advance positions and, in particular, critical political judgments I more readily espouse in my books. My first response is I think these sermons do express my politics, though you will never find me using a sermon to take a political position in terms determined by the political parties of the American political system. But I hope a sermon like "Glory" and calling attention to Barth suggests a way that Christians in America can begin to imagine what difference being a Christian in America should make. I try to avoid any presumption that I am preaching my opinion by keeping the focus on God, and in particular in this sermon, God's glory.

The sermons preached at Christ Church Cathedral are perhaps more philosophical than those for Holy Family. If that is the case I was not intentional about that difference. Rather, I suspect my use of James and Foucault is an attempt to characterize a stance I assume is widely shared though often not articulated. I know, for example, when I delivered "Facing Nothingness—Facing God" I could feel in the congregation a nervous identification with James's perspective. I cannot resist calling attention to the line I discovered as I wrote "Crowd Control," that is, "When you have a mind you have made up, you have become a card-carrying member of the crowd." I hope that is a remark well worth contemplating.

The sermons grouped in "Diverse Occasions" are just that—sermons written for special occasions. A word needs to be said about the context of "Coming Home." In 2010, Jon Pot, the senior editor at Eerdmans, arranged a reception for the release of my memoir *Hannah's Child* to take place at the annual meeting of the Society of Christian Ethics. I was very honored by the presence of Rev. Annelda Crawford, who now serves the church my father built and my family attended as I was growing up in Texas. Rev. Crawford invited me to come to Pleasant Mound-Urban Park to preach and meet old friends. Rev. Crawford is an AfricanAmerican minister whose faith and energy refuses to let Pleasant Mound United Methodist Church die. You do not say "no" to a person like Annelda Crawford. It was a wonderful occasion, and I hope I delivered a sermon that honored my parents and their faithfulness to Christ's Church.

I should also say a word about "Trust" because I suspect many readers will wonder how, given the strong ecclesial emphasis in my work, I can write and deliver a sermon like "Trust." The answer is very simple. As I suggested above, I try never to forget that we are human beings. That this sermon begins with a phenomenology of trust may seem a reversion to some "method of correlation."[16] But what I hope the sermon

---

16. The "method of correlation" is Tillich's phrase for describing the method inherent to his system. The method of correlation is a way to unite message with situation. "It tries to correlate the questions implied in the situation with the answers implied in the message. It does not derive the answers from the questions as a self-defying apologetic theology does. Nor does it elaborate answers without relating them to the questions as a self-defying kerygmatic theology does. It correlates questions and answers, situations and message, human existence and divine manifestation." *Systematic Theology*, Vol. I (Chicago: University of Chicago Press, 1951), 8. For an appreciative critique of this method see David Kelsey, *Eccentric Existence: A Theological Anthropology*, Vol. I (Louisville: Westminster John Knox, 2009), 112–19.

does is show the difference God makes for helping us acknowledge how dependent we are on trust. Rather than the sermon exemplifying a method of any kind, I should like to think that "Trust," as well as most of the sermons in *Without Apology*, exemplify Hans Frei's characterization of Barth's work, that is, as an *ad hoc* apologetics.[17]

The last section, "Sermons on the Priesthood," may seem specialized but I think the reader may find them some of the more engaging sermons in the book. In these sermons I make no attempt to avoid the controversies that currently capture the attention of Christian and non-Christian alike. But I try to reclaim the common life of the church, and the significance of the work of the ministry, to remind us that "we are not dead yet." We are not dead yet because we still have faithful priests who go about their tasks on a daily basis without fanfare and in the name of Christ.

I am not sure how or why it has happened but over the last several years I have been honored to deliver sermons at the graduation services at Virginia Theological Seminary,[18] Eastern Mennonite Seminary,[19] and most recently at the Seminary of the Southwest and Nashotah House. I am profoundly grateful to be

---

17. Hans Frei, *Types of Christian Theology*, ed. George Hunsinger and William Placher (New Haven: Yale University Press, 1992). Frei observes that Barth "will use scriptural exegesis to illustrate his themes; he will do ethics to indicate that this narrated, narratable world is at the same time the ordinary world in which we are responsible for our actions; and he will do *ad hoc* apologetics, in order to throw into relief particular features of this world by distancing them from or approximating them to other descriptions of the same linguistic worlds" (161).

18. The address at Virginia was not officially a sermon, but something like a sermon. It can be found as Appendix C in my book *The State of the University: Academic Knowledges and the Knowledge of God* (Oxford: Blackwell, 2007), 209–14.

19. The sermon at Eastern Mennonite Seminary is titled "Speaking Christian" and is included in my *Working with Words: On Learning to Speak Christian*, 84–93.

given the opportunity to address the graduates of these institutions. After all, I am a layperson. I am acutely aware of how profoundly my life depends on those who are called to the ministry. Accordingly, I try very hard to convey why that is the case not only for me but for the church itself.

I have included three short pieces that are not sermons but commensurate in my view with the purpose of *Without Apology*. "Leadership" was written for the *Duke Divinity School Magazine* and is obviously relevant to issues of ministry. "An Open Letter to Christians Beginning College" was published in *First Things*. I wrote the "Open Letter" because Rusty Reno asked me to write the letter and I try not to say "no" to Rusty. Rusty not only asked me to write the "Open Letter" but his suggestions for what the letter should do, his editing, and his writing made a substantial contribution to the letter. I have included it because I have had so many requests for copies of the letter I thought it should appear somewhere.

The letter urges young Christians going to college to take seriously their intellectual vocation. I should like to think that *Without Apology* takes seriously that admonition for the work of preaching. Christians simply cannot afford to use lazy speech and employ sloppy thinking. The church is privileged and charged Sunday after Sunday to proclaim the Word of God. That Word should force us to think hard and to use words with care. What an extraordinary opportunity we have been given as Christians to stand under the Word of God so that we might learn to speak the truth to one another and to the world. In some small measure, it is my hope that these sermons will be of some help for that task.

Finally, the last piece, "Sexing the Ministry," was written at the request of my friend Patricia Beattie Jung, who was compiling a book on ministerial ethics and health. In it I have tried to say what I take to be the heart of the matter: that ministry can be profoundly lonely and until the church is able to name this we will continue to be marked by "scandals." Again, truthful speech is crucial for a healthier communion, and until our speech about sexuality is recovered within a distinctly Christian grammar we will not be able to speak about sexuality truthfully. This is as important for ministers as for the rest of us.

PART I

Sermons at Church of the Holy Family, Chapel Hill, North Carolina

1

Incarnation

Delivered January 2, 2011

Jeremiah 31:2–14
Psalm 84
Ephesians 1:3–6, 15–19
Luke 2:41–52

I am a theologian. To be a theologian is to have an extremely odd job. It is an odd job, but it is a job I love. One of the reasons I love my job is that I hope in some small way it is a job that makes some contribution to our common life at the Church of the Holy Family. Christians are a people who have a faith that forces people like me to exist. Christians are a people whose faith demands we attempt to understand what we believe. Accordingly theology is an office in the church that some are called to perform. That does not mean that "understanding the faith" is restricted to those who identify themselves as theologians, but by being so identified the church at least knows who is to be held responsible.

I have always been a bit hesitant to say what I do at Holy Family because I am not sure what you make of having a theologian among you. Because theology has become one subject among others in the contemporary university, I fear you may think that a theologian, like academics in other fields, may know something about their subject you do not know. For example, you may think that a theologian is an expert about Christianity or, God help us, even God.

Theologians sometimes encourage you to think they know more about God than you do. They do so because they have a doubtful status in the university. Most of their colleagues in other disciplines in the contemporary university think theology is a subject at best equivalent to witchcraft. One of the ways theologians try to secure some status in the university is to pretend we are really historians who do not necessarily believe in God; rather God is what people we study believe. That strategy seldom works. For the theologian, therefore, to be regarded by Christians as having some authority is reassuring given the lack of status theology has as a university subject.

In truth, however, without the practice of the faith in Jesus Christ by the church, the work of the theologian is unintelligible. Our job is not to know more than those who gather Sunday after Sunday to worship God, but rather our job is to help us all better understand what we do when we are so gathered. The work of the theologian, I think, is not unlike English teachers who insist that the noun and verb agree. English teachers do not make us speak and write English with nouns and verbs. Rather they help us speak and write English well.

Those of us who have felt the fury and scorn of good English teachers because our verb and noun did not agree may sometimes wonder if English teachers do not make a mountain out of a mole hill. We suspect they may do so in an effort to make themselves more important than they are. But English teachers are right to think how we say what we say matters. The work of theology is probably not as important as the work of English teachers, but our work, like theirs, entails attention to grammar.

By now you may well be thinking, "He really is a hopeless academic. He has forgotten that this is supposed to be a sermon rather than a lecture." In truth I often try to defy those categories by preaching when I lecture and lecturing when I preach. But I have not forgotten that this is the Second Sunday of Christmas. I have begun making these general remarks about theology because I hope to show you that our texts demand a certain attention to the grammar of the faith. In particular, they invite us to think about the mystery of the Incarnation.

For example, consider Paul's letter to the Ephesians. After beginning with his usual salutation, he provides a blessing—a thanksgiving—to God, the Father of the Lord Jesus Christ. He continues by noting that we have been blessed in Christ with every spiritual blessing because we have been chosen "in Christ before the foundation of the world to be holy and blameless before him in love" (Ephesians 1:3) According to Paul, we have been destined, elected, adopted from eternity by Jesus Christ to be God's children.

Paul's blessing, a blessing he seems to think is not in any way extraordinary, entails what I can only describe as maximalist Christological claims. Paul assumes that Christ was with God before there was a "was." That Christ was before there was a "was" is a grammatical remark that suggests that Christ is not some subsequent thought God might have had, but rather that whatever it means to say God means we must also say Christ. Unlike us, there is no time when Christ was not.

This reality, i.e., that there was never a time when Christ was not, forced the church to say what we say when we say God is three in one. That is why we say Sunday after Sunday, "We believe in one Lord, Jesus Christ, the only Son of God, eternally begotten of the Father, God from God, Light from Light, true

God from true God, begotten, not made, of one Being with the Father." "Begotten, not made" is a grammatical remark.

The Gospel for this morning is about a twelve-year-old boy who went with his parents to Jerusalem for the festival of the Passover. After the festival was over his parents began their trip home, confident that Jesus was with relatives and friends. Discovering that Jesus was not with relatives or friends, his parents returned to Jerusalem only to find him in the temple expounding Torah with teachers who were amazed at his understanding. Mary was, as we say in the South, "none too pleased" with him.

In fact, we are told, she was astonished, not only by his ability to hold his own with the teachers in the temple, but because he seemed to care so little about how Mary and Joseph would feel once they discovered he was not with relatives and friends. Jesus does not seem the least bit ashamed telling his mother that he must be in the house of his Father, that is, the God of Israel. An extraordinary claim they failed to understand at the time, though we are told Mary treasured "all these things in her heart."

I fear too often sermons on this charming story cannot resist turning the story into a moralistic tale about what a good boy Jesus turned out to be. He turned out to be a good boy because, even though, as he said in the temple, he must be obedient to the one who is the Father of Israel, he went to Nazareth with Joseph and Mary and was obedient to them. Jesus, who as he grew up increased in wisdom, was obedient to his parents. He is, therefore, a model of what every child should be. Do what your parents tell you because Jesus, who was very special, did what his parents would have him do.

That is not, however, how Christians in the early church read this story. Rather they wanted to know how Christ, whom

Paul claimed was with God before there was a was, could be the Jesus who thought it more important to interact with the teachers in the temple than to join Mary and Joseph as they made their way back to Nazareth. How strange. The love that moves the sun and the stars is fully present in this boy. Though the Apostles' Creed, because it is a creed for our baptisms, moves from the birth of Jesus to suffering under Pontius Pilate, the church could not forget, because of this text, that Jesus was a boy who had to grow up like any child.

When you have texts like today's reading from Ephesians and a story like this story from Luke, you begin to understand why I suggested above that theology is a discipline forced on the church. We have a faith that forces you to reason about what makes us who we are. The most decisive challenges concerning the truth of what we believe as Christians does not come from outside our faith, that is, from those who do not share our convictions, but from within. Accordingly, the early church had no time for moralistic questions about how to get our children to do what we want them to do. Rather, the challenge was how the church could believe that the Christ, who was there before there was a beginning, could be the same Jesus who had to grow up.

In truth, we are never quite sure what we believe until someone gets it wrong. That is why those we call heretics are so blessed because without them we would not know what we believe. In this case, a bishop in Laodicea named Apollinaris could not believe that the one who is "true God from true God," "begotten not made," could be fully God and fully a little boy. Accordingly, he thought Jesus had human flesh and soul, but his mind, the Logos, was divine. Therefore he argued that when Jesus says he must be in his Father's house, he is speaking with the rational faculty that is of one Being with the Father.

Yet that would mean that he was not really a twelve-year-old boy. Many worried if he was not a twelve-year-old boy, if he did not need to "increase in wisdom and in years," then our salvation would be in doubt. Theologians like Gregory of Nazianzus pointed out that surely our minds need redeeming so Jesus must share our rational nature. As Gregory put it, "what was not assumed cannot be saved."

After much debate (a debate lasting a century), the church, at the Fourth Ecumenical Council at Chalcedon, in the year 451, declared that our Lord Jesus Christ is "truly God and truly man," being of two natures "without confusion, without change, without division, without separation; the distinction of natures being in no way annulled by the union." Chalcedon did not "solve" or explain how this Jesus was at once fully God and fully human, but the fathers at Chalcedon gave us the parameters necessary for how we can continue to explore this mystery, the mystery of the Incarnation, that is the center of our faith.

After Chalcedon, however, Christians no longer could read the scripture as if Jesus was God when he declared he must be in his Father's house but human when he was obedient to his mother and father. Jesus was not fifty percent God here and fifty percent human there, but in everything he was one hundred percent God and one hundred percent human. Which means for those who worship this man, we cannot help but be forced to reconsider whether we know what we say when we say "God."

Thus the creation of that strange activity called theology. How extraordinary. You, the people of God, think it important to ask some to do nothing with their lives but to think about what we say when we say "God." God knows those so set aside often make mistakes, tempted as we are to take pride in what we do by assuming we are more important than we are. But then we are humbled by the One about whom we think, that is, the One who became for us fully human so that we might share in God's very life.

For what we do know is that if Jesus is not fully God and fully human, then we can make no sense of the Eucharist. This wine and this bread is the food we need to sustain human life. Just as God joined God's life with the life of Jesus without ceasing to be God, so we receive now the very body and blood of Christ without this bread and wine ceasing to be bread and wine. So receiving, moreover, we become for the world, in the language of Jeremiah, "a watered garden," witnesses to God's abundance.

Because Jesus is very God and very man, at the Eucharist we are consumed by what we consume. God became human, assumed our nature, so that we might share in God's very life. The Eastern Church has a name for this transformation. It is called *theosis* and it means we only are able to be fully human to the extent we are divinized. A heady claim but one we live out at Holy Family every time we share in this meal. How extraordinary it turns out the ordinary is—a twelve-year-old is God's Son. Worship him!

2

Glory

Delivered July 24, 2011

1 Kings 3:5–12
Psalm 119:129–136
Romans 8:26–39
Matthew 13:31–33, 44–52

In 1922, in the mountain village of Safenwil, Switzerland, an unknown pastor with no academic standing unleashed on the world his commentary on Paul's epistle to the Romans. The book would later be described as a bomb tossed into the playground of theologians. The description was well-earned because the author challenged the reigning theological presumption of the day, that is, that thought or speech about God is first and foremost thought and speech about what it means to be human. According to the author of this commentary, modern theologians thought they were speaking of God if they spoke about being human in a very loud voice.

The commentary's author was Karl Barth. Barth, who would never receive a Ph.D., arguably became the most significant theologian of the last century. His critique of the reigning theological paradigm generally known as Protestant liberalism, a position that dominated Protestant theological faculties in Germany where Barth was educated, was occasioned by Barth's dismay that the most prominent theologians in Germany, his teachers, had signed a manifesto in 1914 supporting the kaiser's war policy.

Barth was shocked by their support of the war because he assumed that the liberal convictions of his teachers and their allies would prevent their advocacy of German war aims. Advocates of Protestant liberalism had sought to reconstruct Christian beliefs in response to the challenges represented by developments in the sciences and the discipline of history, particularly as the latter had implications for Biblical interpretation. Theologians presumed that if Christian theological claims could be defended, they must underwrite the achievements of history associated with the economic and political developments that they assumed expressed the fulfillment of the highest human aspirations. From such a theological perspective, to be a Christian was equivalent to the belief that it is up to us to make history come out right. Thus from the point of view of the theologians who supported the war, Germany was the embodiment of such a history.

In his commentary on Paul's letter to the Romans, Barth gave expression to what he described as the "strange new world of the Bible." What he discovered, what he expressed in dramatic fashion, was that the subject of the Bible is God's glory. With prose burning with passion, Barth wrote:

> The hope of His glory emerges for us when nothing but the existentiality of God remains, and He becomes to us the veritable and living God. He, whom we can apprehend only as against us, stands there—for us. That Christ, who deprives us of everything but the existentiality of God, has been delivered up, means—we must dare to say it, dare to storm the fortress which is impregnable—and already captured!—that *God is for us* (8:31), and we are by His side. Christ who has been *delivered up* in the Spirit, the Truth, the restless arm of

God. "If so be that we suffer with Him, how can it be that we should not also be glorified with Him (8:17)?"[1]

Barth's discovery that God is God and we are not, that a hope that is visible is not hope, that direct talk of God cannot be talk of the living God, was received by American theologians as a retreat from responsible intellectual and social engagement. Yet it was Karl Barth who lost his chair in the faculty of theology at the University of Bohn because he refused to take the oath of obedience to Hitler. It was Karl Barth who early on recognized the demonic character of the Nazi movement and organized opposition to Hitler's attempt to create the German Christian Church. That opposition took the form of the Barmen Declaration where Barth wrote: "We reject the false doctrine, as though there were areas of our life in which we would not belong to Jesus Christ, but to other Lords—areas in which we would not need justification and sanctification through him." Barth's ability to see through Hitler's alleged support of the church, moreover, had everything to do with his discovery that Paul's letter to the Romans has at its center, as Paul says earlier in the letter, that our hope is in the sharing of "the glory of God" (Romans 5:2).

I suspect most of us assume that if we had been citizens of Germany in 1933 we would have been able to identify Hitler and his party for the thugs they no doubt were. But good people, people like you and me, supported Hitler because he represented the attempt to recover the glory of Germany from the ruins of their defeat in World War I.

I have begun with this brief history of Barth's commentary on Romans to help us recognize what an unsettling text we have before

---

1. Karl Barth, *The Epistle to the Romans* (Oxford: University Press, 1968), 327.

us. We know this passage all too well. We know it well because we hear it often at funerals. "Who can separate us from the love of God in Christ Jesus our Lord"—not death nor life, not angels, not rulers, not things present nor things to come, not powers, not height nor depth, not anything else in all creation. Words rightly used to comfort us while facing the death of those we love. But these words can tempt us to forget that it is not just death that threatens to separate us from the God who has found us in Christ Jesus our Lord. Rather these other things we take to be goods, i.e., life, angels, rulers, and powers, can also threaten to come between Christ and his church.

By suggesting this text should unsettle us, I mean to call attention to the radical political implications entailed by our hope of sharing the glory of God. To share in the glory of God is to be drawn near to God by acknowledging that God has first drawn near to us. The otherness of God that Barth identified in his commentary on Romans is the God of love whose distance from us is constituted by what Barth was later to call "the humanity of God." God's glory has been made present to us in Christ Jesus, which decisively puts an end to all of our attempts to make God a god of our own devising.

It is so tempting to read Paul, as many of the great representatives of the liberal Protestant enterprise did and as some who now think of themselves as religiously conservative do, to confirm what we think being human is about. "We know all things work together for good" too often is used to justify what is taken to be progress or to recommend patience in the face of difficulty. But Paul says all things work for good for those who love God. Paul then observes that such a good may mean that those who enjoy that good may suffer hardship, distress, persecution, famine, nakedness, peril, or the sword. That list should surely make us think twice about wanting the good made possible by all things working together. Is it any wonder that Paul suggests that we do not know how to pray as we ought?

Yet, according to Paul, the good news is that those whom God predestined he also called, those whom he called he also justified, and those whom he justified he also glorified. Yet what does it mean to be glorified? We often sing or say:

> Glory to God in the highest,
> and peace to his people on earth.
>
> Lord God, heavenly King,
> Almighty God and Father,
> we worship you, we give you thanks,
> we praise you for your glory.

That we do so is surely right, but I suspect we may well have lost the significance of what it means to celebrate God's glory and our reflection of that glory. We say God is the greatest *this* or the most powerful *that*, so to praise God for God's glory just seems to be another attribution that does little work. Yet to praise God for God's glory is, as Barth insists, to be reminded that divine glory consists in God's self-glorification. God's glory is the glory of the divine Trinity in which God's radiance manifests God's lively desire to love and be loved by us.

The Psalmist prays, "Make your face shine upon your servant." Seeing God face to face is a frightful prospect, yet it seems we should pray so that we might glow with the radiance of God's glory. For the living God is the source of all light. God's glory is the glory of creation, for the whole point of creation is that God desires to have a reflection of the glory that is the very life of the Trinity. Such a God is capable of giving his only Son to die on a cross only to be raised to sit in glory at the Father's right hand so that we might be justified and thus reflect God's glory.

Our glory, therefore, is God's glory as shown through the life, death, resurrection, and ascension of Jesus Christ. This means that the glory of God entails a politics with death at its center. It is a politics well diagnosed by Augustine, who contrasted the Christian understanding of what it means for us to reflect the glory of God with the Roman desire for glory. According to Augustine, it is the martyrs who exemplify what it means for us to be glorified. The martyrs endured what was inflicted on them because they sought not their own glory but only to reflect the glory of the One who endured and triumphed through cross and resurrection. The martyrs did not try to guarantee that they would be remembered and glorified by the standards provided by the world. Yet the martyrs quite literally glow, radiate a light so brilliant it cannot be denied, because the light that enlightens them is that which is but a reflection of God's glory.

By contrast the Romans did what was regarded as good because they hoped to receive "glory from their fellow men."[2] Before you become too critical of the Roman desire for glory, think how pathetic in contrast to their desire for glory is our desire for fame. For example, Augustine observes that the desire for glory could lead some citizens of Rome to sacrifice their material well-being and even their lives for the common good. Indeed, Augustine acknowledged that Romans, in their desire for glory, might even resist the temptation to avarice, succumb to no sensual indulgence, and pursue their country's well-being in the hope of acquiring power and honor. Yet Augustine

---

2. Augustine, *City of God*, V, 19, trans. David Knowles (Middlesex, England: Penguin, 1977), 212.

observes that their desperate attempt to defeat death by ensuring their glory would persist after death could not help but be frustrated by the knowledge that those who would remember their glory would, in their turn, die.

Some Romans thought there was an alternative. If they could not ensure their glorification, they could try to make the glory of Rome eternal. But the effort to make Rome eternal meant Romans had to impose on others the threat and reality of death to ensure the continued existence of Rome. Rome was not the first to employ this hopeless strategy, but many have subsequently followed her example. And the rest, I fear, is history.

But it is not *our* history. Our history—Christian history— is the history of the kingdom of God. This observation is precisely what Barth was trying to help us see. And this is what today's Gospel reading teaches us. The kingdom of heaven is where God makes God's glory manifest. Although it may be the tiniest seed—the tiniest granule of yeast—once received, God's glory shines forth, creating new life where there was none. As Christians, we believe our history is the history of those "predestined to be conformed to the image of his Son, in order that he might be the firstborn within a large family" (Romans 8:29). Those so born may be "killed all day long" (Romans 8:36), but, though they kill us, they cannot determine the meaning of our deaths. As with the martyrs, the meaning of any saint's life and death comes from their citizenship in the kingdom of heaven, which is but a manifestation of God's own glory.

I am well aware that you may be thinking, "What does this have to do with us?" We are not martyrs. At least, we are not martyrs—yet. I will grant you this, but we *are* a church that remembers martyrs. That is no small thing. Moreover, if we let our imaginations take us beyond this nation's borders we

will see that the contemporary church continues to produce
martyrs. Today there are sisters and brothers who are suffering
death for the sake of the cross of Jesus Christ. And the glory
that shines forth from these witnesses is the glory that, God
help us, enables us to see future Hitlers, and all the anti-Christs,
for what they are—that is, murderous tyrants who feed on our
fear of death.

God is God and we are not, but the God that we are not is
the God who would glorify us through his Son. May we ever be a
people who rejoice and sing:

> For you alone are the Holy One,
> you alone are the Lord,
> you alone are the Most High,
>> Jesus Christ,
>> with the Holy Spirit,
>> in the glory of God the Father. Amen.

3

Tenderness

Maundy Thursday
Delivered April 5, 2012

Exodus 12:1–4, 5–14
Psalm 116:1, 10–17
1 Corinthians 11:23–26
John 13:1–17, 31–35

This is Maundy Thursday. We are going to wash one another's feet. What have we gotten ourselves into? We are Episcopalians. We do not come to church to be touched. We are willing to shake hands at the passing of peace, and maybe even give one another an occasional hug, but that is about as much touching we can stand. At least, that is about as much touching we can stand when we are in church.

Yet tonight we are asked to wash one another's feet. Thank God, we only have to do this once a year. Some Anabaptists, that is, Mennonites and other weird people, do it multiple times in the year. But we know they are "different." We are not sure how they are different but we know they are not Episcopalians. Rather, they are people who think that washing feet is possibly as important as the Eucharist; or better put, they think in the Gospel of John the institution of the Lord's Supper is inseparable from foot-washing. It is, in fact, a very interesting question, why the washing of feet did not become a sacrament because, like baptism and Eucharist, we are commanded by Jesus to wash one another's feet.

Although I may be a neophyte Episcopalian, I find myself on the Episcopal side of these matters. I am more or less ready to wash someone's feet, but, like Peter, I discover I am not prepared to have my feet washed. I am willing to play like I am a servant and wash the feet of someone else. When I wash the feet of someone else I am still in control. But to have someone wash my feet makes me feel vulnerable. My feet are not all that attractive and they are usually covered up. To ask me to take off my socks feels like I am being asked to expose myself. It makes me feel distinctly uncomfortable and I am not at all sure I like what we are about to do.

To have someone wash my feet, moreover, is an act of intimacy. We are asked by the one kneeling before us, "May I wash your feet?" Who is this person willing to wash my feet? I may not even know his or her name. I am supposed to enthusiastically say, "Yes, by all means wash my feet." But that means he or she will have to touch me. Dear God, how did I get myself into this predicament? I did not come to church to be served, to be cared for, by someone else. Yet here I am, stuck in this communal rite that requires some acknowledgment on my part that this is a practice worth doing. This is not going to be easy.

Yet, I think it right that what we are about to do is not easy. Jean Vanier, in his remarkable book *Drawn into the Mystery of Jesus through the Gospel of John*, observes that Peter's first reaction to Jesus' declaration that he will wash the disciples' feet is perfectly understandable. Like us, Peter presumes (a very human presumption) that Jesus is superior, the Lord and Master, which means he should never wash the feet of the disciples. It is for us to wash his feet, not for him to wash our feet.

Peter assumes, Vanier observes, that all societies are built on the model of a pyramid in which our relations to one another are determined by diverse hierarchies. By washing the feet of his disciples, Vanier suggests, Jesus enacts a new community not determined by hierarchy but by the body. That is, just as our individual body needs its particular parts, so we as the body of Christ need one another. We are a bodily community in which every person has a place, whatever our abilities or disabilities, and by which we accordingly depend on one another. It is good that Clarke, Michelle, and Paula wash our feet, but it is just as important that their feet be washed by us.

Commenting on Peter's response, "Not only my feet but my hands and my head," Vanier observes that Peter still fails to understand what Jesus is doing. Peter does not understand that the washing of feet is not an isolated action but the very heart of the new creation enacted by Christ. It is an action constitutive of the message of love seen most clearly in Jesus' suggestion that if we are to enter into the kingdom we have to become like little children who have been "born" from on high. When we wash one another's feet, we make Jesus present so that a people are created, a body is born, in which the weakest member is not excluded. To wash one another's feet is to recall the waters of baptism through which we die to sin and are reborn into Christ.

We should not be surprised that foot-washing is a central act for the movement Jean Vanier began known as L'Arche. It is a movement in which homes are established wherein some designated as mentally disabled learn to live with those not so designated. In L'Arche, to wash a person's feet is an action that creates and expresses a communion of hearts. Vanier reports that when he left the leadership of his community, he lived a sabbatical year in one of the homes that welcomes people with severe handi-caps. Among them was Eric, who had been sent to live at L'Arche when the local psychiatric hospital gave up on him. He was six-teen. He was blind, deaf, he could not walk or speak, and he was not toilet trained. He was in anguish, wanting only to die.

Vanier observes that Eric, like many who come to L'Arche homes, was broken because he sensed he was a disappointment for his parents. That these L'Arche members are not wanted as they are makes them feel they are no good. Not loved, they think and feel they are, in fact, not loveable. The task of L'Arche was to help transform Eric's broken image of himself into one through which he could recover his value, his beauty, his importance. That transformation was enacted in Eric through touch, through the way he was held as his body was washed. Eric learned he was precious, making him capable of love, making him capable of touching and loving others.

That is why Vanier suggests that he is most deeply moved when someone with disabilities washes his feet. It is the ultimate act of tenderness. In the washing of feet, there is a tenderness and intimacy we cannot help but fear, threatening, as it does, to expose our presumption that if you really knew me you could not love me. Jesus washing the feet of his disciples, like the cru-cifixion itself, is an act of tenderness. It is an act in which all attempts to protect ourselves from tenderness are defeated. For it is through such tenderness we are saved. Through such tender-ness we learn to accept our own quite particular forms of poverty and weakness. And in the process we learn our vulnerability is a strength, enabling us to cry out: "I cannot do this on my own! I need your help."

And Jesus washed Judas's feet. He knew Judas would betray him. Judas failed to believe the world would be saved by such tenderness. Yet Jesus washed Judas's feet. What Peter, under the guidance of the Holy Spirit, was later to understand is that this kingdom of forgiveness extends even to Judas. For a new community has been created and is renewed as we become capable of loving one another as Jesus has loved us. So come, let us wash and be washed so that the world might know its salvation is not won or merited, but given by a loving God who humbled himself so that we might be touched and touch one another.

4

Saints

All Saints Day
Delivered November 4, 2012

Wisdom of Solomon 3:1–9
Psalm 24
Revelation 21:1–6a
John 11:32–44

Dorothy Day, the founder of the Catholic Worker, a movement committed to providing a place for the homeless to sleep, to feeding the hungry, and to ending war, when told some were planning a campaign to have her made a saint is said to have responded, "You are not going to get rid of me that easily." Day's response, a quite understandable response, reflects the widespread presumption that saints are very, very holy people. That they are very, very holy people suggests, moreover, that saints rise above all conflict and controversy.

Dorothy Day, an extremely pious convert to Catholicism, was not about to let her life be so understood. She was a fighter against injustice. She challenged the presumption that we, and particularly the rich, could do what we want with our money. She was often arrested because of her active protest against war. If holiness meant that saints were above the fray, then Day certainly did not want to be a saint. Dorothy Day, who died in 1980 and is now in the process the Catholic Church has developed for discerning saints, was a very tough lady whose toughness was made necessary by her gentle love of Christ and the poor.

I call attention to Dorothy Day to remind us that our assumptions about what makes a saint a saint often fail to attend to the extraordinary diversity of people the church has named as saints. Paul begins his letter to the Ephesians, as well as his second letter to the Corinthians, by addressing all the members of those churches as "the saints who are faithful in Christ Jesus." Paul seems to have assumed being a Christian and being a saint were one and the same. That assumption no doubt reflected Paul's presumption that to be a Christian meant you were ready to die for the faith.

When the church came under persecution in the first centuries following the death of Jesus, saints began to be identified with those who were martyrs. Saints, therefore, not only were killed rather than be unfaithful to Christ but they often died like him. After Roman persecution came to an end, many Christians found another form of life they thought to be in continuity with martyrdom: the slow martyrdom of the ascetical life in which one dies to sin so that Christ might live. Such an understanding of sainthood shares with the martyrs a refusal to compromise with worldly powers. It is no wonder that given the identification of sainthood with both martyrs and ascetics, Christians increasingly came to assume that saints live extraordinary—almost beyond belief—lives.

That martyrs and ascetics are considered holy does not mean, however, that they are not tough and often difficult people. They are very tough and oftentimes very difficult to get along with. Just ask yourself—would you really want to have Saint Paul for a friend? Paul's unrelenting passion for the Gospel, his unwillingness to compromise, his judgmental attitude about how we should live, his refusal to let the threat of death deter his mission, I suspect would, for many of us, make him a rather tiresome companion. Paul does not seem to understand that most of us have to get on with the everyday business of life. Or consider Saint Francis. We celebrate his preaching to the birds, but his rigorous commitment to poverty was, at the time, seen for what it was—that is, a profound challenge to the riches of the church.

Often it is non-Christians who best understand how threatening those we Christians identify as saints may be. Rome did not persecute and kill Christians for no reason. Of course, in the earliest years of the life of the church, Christians were not on the Roman radar screen. Christians were not numerous, and they were largely from social and economic classes of little or no significance, which meant the Roman elites had little reason to recognize their existence. If Christians were noticed by the Romans, it was but one more instance of the variety of weird people that were the result of Roman conquest. Christians were no threat to Rome, though they worshiped someone who had been killed by Rome.

In the second century, Christians were noticed by Pliny, an upper class Roman official who served under Emperor Trajan. Pliny found Christians hard to understand but reported to Trajan that as far as he could tell they were but one of the countless clubs organized to deal with issues of common concern. These clubs were not only numerous but diverse, often organized around commercial and property interests. Some of these associations were funerary societies whose purpose was to provide burial expenses for members who had died as well as ensuring that the dead received a decent burial. Pliny reported to Trajan that the Christians were some form of a burial society.

Pliny's characterization of the church as a burial society was not quite right, but it is surprisingly accurate. We are a burial society if, as is certainly the case, baptism is the heart of our life together. For it is surely the case that we are a people who refuse to let death determine our relation to one another. Through baptism we are made participants in the communion of saints, which means we refuse to let the power of death determine our ongoing relation with those who have made our lives possible. We happily remember the saints and through that memory we are made participants in that great communion that surrounds God's throne.

A people constituted by such a memory could not help but come into conflict with Rome. Christians refused Rome's presumption that the only memory that mattered was how you were remembered by eternal Rome. There were many reasons Christians were eventually killed by Rome, not the least being the church's challenge to the Roman presumption that only Rome could determine the significance of life. The Christian challenge only intensified and confounded the Romans who simply could not comprehend that Rome could not defeat the Christians by killing them.

Of course Christians well understood that Rome had power over life and death, but the very fact that the Christian dead were called martyrs meant Rome had lost. To be a martyr, to be a saint, meant Rome could kill Christians for being Christian but Rome could not determine the meaning of their deaths. The meaning of their deaths, the meaning of our deaths, is determined in baptism. That Christians could be "happily remembered" by the church was the ultimate challenge to Rome. To be so remembered means these lives are constituted by a narrative in which Christ is at the center.

Put differently, it is important to remember that the martyr and saint cannot know they are a martyr or a saint on their own. They only know they are a martyr or saint when God, and the church in obedience to God, tells them who they are. Listen again to the marvelous passage from the Wisdom of Solomon:

> But the souls of the righteous are in the hand of God,
> and no torment will ever touch them.
> In the eyes of the foolish they seemed to have died,
> and their departure was thought to be a disaster,
> and their going from us to be their destruction;
> but they are at peace.
> For though in the sight of others they were punished,
> their hope is full of immortality.
> Having been disciplined a little, they will receive great good,
> because God tested them and found them worthy
>   of himself;
> like gold in the furnace he tried them,
> and like a sacrificial burnt offering he accepted them.
> In the time of their visitation they will shine forth,
> and will run like sparks through the stubble.
> They will govern nations and rule over peoples,
> and the Lord will reign over them forever.
> Those who trust in him will understand truth,
> and the faithful will abide with him in love,
> because grace and mercy are upon his holy ones,
> and he watches over his elect.

> (Wisdom of Solomon 3:1–9)

This passage from the Wisdom of Solomon applies not only to martyrs and saints, it describes all of us. None of us know who we are until God tells us. That we only discover who we are when God tells us is why, as we learn from our sainted martyrs, we may be killed but we cannot be victimized. Victims, even if they have been in some sense liberated, remain captive just to the extent they continue to think of themselves as victims. To continue to think of oneself as a victim lets the oppressor win. As Christians we refuse to let our enemies determine who we are because we have learned to recognize ourselves first and foremost through the communion of saints. Holiness is shorthand for saying we have been saved by being made part of an extraordinary community that refuses to let the oppressor determine who we are.

That is why Christians under persecution often gathered to worship God at the tombs of the martyrs. They did so because, just as the lives and deaths of the martyrs witnessed to the life of Christ, so Christians believed that by drawing near the martyrs, they drew near to heaven itself. Thus the inscription on the tomb of Martin of Tours reads: "Here lies Martin the bishop, of holy memory, whose soul is in the hand of God; but he is fully here, present and made plain in the miracles of every kind." They clung to Martin because they believed he was a person of power who would protect them from those who would persecute them. The protection Martin provided was real, offering as it must the possibility that even their persecutors might be reconciled to God.

By now I assume it is obvious that the celebration of All Saints is a celebration of the lives and deaths of those who have gone before. It is not by accident that our scripture passages for this morning are death-determined. The "All" of All Saints is the acknowledgment by the church that we do not know the names of all those who have lived and died to make possible what we are about to do, that is, baptize these children into the death and resurrection of Christ. We do not know, but we hope that those we baptize on this day will not be persecuted or killed for what we are about to do to them. But we also know that even if they have to suffer for the faith they will be surrounded by that throng of saints, saints like Dorothy Day, Martin of Tours, and Paul the Apostle, who make up the tough and difficult people we know populate that great multitude called the communion of saints.

PART II

Sermons at Christ Church Cathedral, Nashville, Tennessee

5

Letting Go

Delivered October 3, 2010

Habakkuk 1:1–6, 12–13; 2:1–4
Psalm 37:1–18
2 Timothy 1:6–14
Luke 17:5–10

The contingency, the shear unpredictability, of life frustrates and maddens us. We find ourselves in situations in which we are sure that if we do not do X, then Y will happen; but after we have done X, it turns out that Z was the result. Because Z was the result, we are not even sure if what we did in the first place was X. For example, I am sure many of you by now are beginning to wonder what you did when you called Timothy Kimbrough to be dean of Christ Church Cathedral. You may have thought you knew what you were doing but I have a hunch you got more than you bargained for.

Of course it is a two-way street. Timothy may have thought he knew what he was doing when he came to Christ Church, but I suspect he has discovered that what he thought he was doing does not correspond to what he did. We live our lives prospectively, but it turns out that we only know what we have done retrospectively. And it may be that we only know what we have done retrospectively when it is too late to do anything about it. If you do not believe that I ask you to reflect on whether you

knew what you were doing when you chose your major in college, your profession, or to marry or not to marry.

It is one thing to acknowledge that we may not be in control
of our personal lives, but it is quite another thing to recognize
that our lack of control also applies to that larger world we call
politics. We are told that if we do not infuse the economy, whatever that is, with stimulus money, then a depression cannot be
avoided. We have not had a depression, so what we did must have
worked. The only problem with that line of reasoning is that you
cannot show a causal relation by something not happening. Yet,
those we have endowed with authority have to claim they know
what they are doing because if they did not know what they were
doing, they should not be in positions of power.

The public policy of our government is one thing, but think
what the unpredictable character of life means in international
affairs. Again, we are often told that we must continue this or
that war because if we do not it will only invite our enemy to
do X or Y, but because we continue the war, our enemy claims
they must do X or Y. Yet lives are being sacrificed so those who
make these decisions, because they are morally good people,
must insist, and indeed must believe, that they know what they
are doing. And we, because we are morally good people, want
to believe that those who lead the most powerful nation in the
world must know what they are doing.

John Howard Yoder, a Mennonite theologian, has observed
that one way to characterize the attitude of those who constitute
this time called "modern" is that we are obsessed with the meaning and direction of history. Whether a given action is right or
not, we believe, will be determined by the effects it produces. As
a result, we are desperate, in Yoder's memorable phrase, to "get a
handle on history." We need a handle on history because we are

determined to make history come out right. This conviction is so deeply founded in our souls, we ignore or repress the fact that there is little evidence to support our presumption that we can be in control of our lives—much less the history of nations.

Yet we are undeterred. We are determined to show that the contingent, the temporal, can be subject to our will. Whatever it may mean to be modern surely must, at the very least, entail our refusal to be determined, to be fated, by the past. We can make a difference. We can be in control. We can defeat contingency. We even have an institution dedicated to that task. It is called the university. In the university are enshrined modes of rationality dedicated to the proposition: If we get better at what we are doing, we may be able to get out of life alive.

That we would like to have a "handle on history" should make us quite sympathetic with the oracle of the prophet Habakkuk. Habakkuk, a contemporary of Jeremiah, cannot understand why the Lord is going to let the Chaldeans, of all people, get away with murder. They are mighty warriors to be sure, but why should might make right? That is not the way it is supposed to work, particularly if Israel is the promised people, the beloved, of God. Not only does it seem that the wicked are winning, but Habakkuk quite reasonably complains that he has to watch the wicked get away with what they are doing and he is not able to do anything about it. But he is a prophet, so, like a watchman, he stations himself on the rampart, awaiting God's reply to his complaint.

God does reply. The Lord commands Habakkuk to "write the vision" plainly on tablets that even those in a hurry can read what is written. The Lord declares that there is a vision that will be fulfilled at the appointed time. The vision is of an end time that God promises will come in due time. But the end that is coming in truth will require those who trust in God to wait. Those who refuse to wait, the proud, may seem to prosper but they will, as our Psalmist reminds us, wither like the grass. In contrast, the righteous will live by their faith.

What could that possibly mean? Does faith mean that though life may seem to be just one damn thing after another, there really is a pattern of purpose that ultimately will make sense? Does faith mean that, though history may seem to be a tale told by an idiot finally signifying nothing, God does have a plan we do not yet fathom? What about the Chaldeans? The wicked may wither like grass, but that is not exactly comforting as long as they are winning. What about the exile? What about the betrayal by the one alone I thought I could trust? What about death?

The righteous may live by faith, but like the apostles in the Gospel for today, given the unpredictability of our lives, we can only ask, "Increase our faith." That seems like a reasonable request. After all, faith is a good thing. But Jesus is not in the least sympathetic with the request. Rather, he says: You have all the faith you need, even though it is as small as the size of a mustard seed.

A mustard seed? Dear God, I wish Jesus had found a better analogy. Preachers have not been able to resist expanding on Jesus' comparison of faith to a mustard seed by suggesting that a small seed can produce a very large plant. So they claim that if you fervently believe the impossible, God will reward your faith by making what you believe a reality. If what you fervently believe does not become a reality, then that is a sign that you did not believe fervently enough. In an interesting way, this line of reasoning can be just another attempt to use faith to give us a handle on history—or at least our lives.

Jesus' refusal to meet the apostles' request to increase their faith is not a judgment about the status of the apostles' subjectivity. The apostles have all they need to live as servants in God's kingdom not because of their ardent belief but because they have Jesus. Jesus is the vision that the Lord told Habakkuk would come at the appointed time. How extraordinary that our God, the Lord, becomes one of us, subject to the same contingencies to which we are subject. Who could have anticipated that God does not disdain the finite, willing even to show up in the womb of Mary? Who could have predicted that our Lord would be willing to be subject to our desperate fears and desires? Even willing to die because of the indecision of a minor Roman official named Pilate?

Jesus refuses to increase the apostles' faith because they have in him all they need to live in a world out of control. For, it turns out, to follow Jesus is ongoing training for learning to live out of control. Faith is but a word for letting go of our presumption that we have to make history come out right. History has come out right. We have seen the end in Jesus. That end makes possible our ability to go on when we are not even sure we know where we are. What we do know is that through cross and resurrection, Jesus defeated the powers that deceptively promise to save us from death by our willingness to coerce and even kill our neighbors.

As one committed to Christian nonviolence, I am often asked: What would you do in X or Y circumstances? The question is meant to make a commitment to nonviolence problematic by suggesting to be committed to nonviolence might result in unacceptable harm to others. Yet too often those who ask such a question assume our lives are mechanistically determined, forgetting that who we are can make a difference. To be sure, that does not mean that everything will "come out all right," but it does mean that a world at war can know a people exist who are an alternative to war.

To learn to let go, to live out of control, does not mean our lives will be free of suffering. Consider Paul. As usual, he is in jail. Yet he writes to Timothy gratefully thanking God for his ancestors who worshiped God with a clear conscience. Paul is not the least embarrassed that he is a follower of Christ because of the promises, promises like those made to Habakkuk, made to his ancestors. Accordingly, Paul reminds Timothy that he is a Christian because of the sincere faith of his grandmother, Lois, and the subsequent faith of Eunice, his mother. Timothy is a Christian because of the faith of his mothers, but that is the way it works for all of us. Grace is the word we have been given to acknowledge that chance, the chance of having a mother called Eunice, is not chance at all but the form God's love for us takes. If you want, you can call that "providence."

That Paul knows God has so determined his life means he does not hesitate to invite Timothy to join him "in suffering for the gospel" (2 Timothy 1:8). Learning to suffer is extended training necessary to rely on the power of God. It is only against this background that we rightly understand Paul's condemnation of works of righteousness. Works, in contrast to faith, is the form our impatience takes. Refusing to believe that we have seen the end in Jesus, we think we must take matters in our hands to make history come out right. But Paul reminds Timothy, and us, that Christ, the immortal One, has abolished death, thereby making it possible for us to live joyfully in a world out of control.

Please note Paul is not a stoic. Paul is not recommending that, given our inability to subject the world to our will, the best course of life is to accept our fate. We are not fated because the world has been redeemed by the life, death, and resurrection of Jesus. Through that life and through that death we have been given a way to live that frees us from being determined by our desperate attempts to be in control. In short, Christ has made it possible for us to take the time in an impatient world to engage in the small gestures of kindness that defy the presumption that if we are to survive, we are fated to live lives of cruelty. Paul indicates this may well mean that Christians will from time to time end up in jail, but there is no shame in that.

That faith means learning to let go, to live out of control, is one of the gifts God gives us to recognize that we cannot do this alone. The tender relationship between Paul and Timothy, I think, is not accidental. Timothy obviously depends on Paul, but the very fact that Timothy exists clearly helps sustain Paul. To learn to live out of control means we must learn to depend on others who are also learning to live out of control. The name given such a people is church. A people so constituted may appear absurd to those determined to make organizations "work." But hopefully they will also think those absurd people are happy.

The contingent and unpredictable character of our lives maddens us. Yet we worship a Lord who did not despise the contingent, becoming unpredictably one of us. The love that moves the sun and the stars turned up in Palestine of all places, only to die on a cross in AD 33. Through those contingent events we have been given everything we need to live out of control in a world desperate for control. To so live means we must learn to trust God and one another. That is why, I assume, we are here at this time and in this place. For at this time and this place, we eat and drink again with the One who makes it possible to live joyfully because we are not afraid of being surprised.

Christ Church Cathedral did call Timothy Kimbrough to be your dean. Like Paul you will need Timothy if you are to be Christ's church, but it is equally true that Timothy will need you to be his Paul if he is to be for you the priest Christ means him to be. That you need one another, I take to be an indication you are a people out of control. Praise God for that.

6

Prisoners No More

Delivered February 13, 2011

Ecclesiasticus 15:15–20
Psalm 119:1–8
1 Corinthians 3:1–9
Matthew 5:21–37

In his extraordinary book *Discipline and Punish: The Birth of the Prison*, Michel Foucault challenges the presumption that the use of modern prisons as a mode of punishment is more humane than past uses of torture. Foucault begins his book with a horrific account of the burning and quartering in 1757 of a man named Damiens who was being punished for plotting to kill the king. Foucault does so to make clear he does not underestimate the cruelty of torture. But Foucault is intent on helping us see how the development of prisons, which are allegedly an alternative to torture, can obscure how we continue to punish bodies; the only difference is that now we do so in a manner that hides from us the cruelty involved.

In particular Foucault calls attention to the great representative of the Enlightenment, the utilitarian philosopher Jeremy Bentham, who sought to reform prisons in the hope that those imprisoned might be punished in a manner that would lead to their reform. Bentham thought the way to do this was to build prisons on the model of a Panopticon. The prison would be a circular or eight-sided building in which each prisoner would have a cell. The external wall would be solid with perhaps only a high window providing some back lighting. The front of the cell would consist only of bars making any privacy for the prisoner impossible.

A tower would be in the middle of the prison in which a guard could constantly observe the prisoners. The genius of Bentham's prison is that the guard in the tower could not see all the prisoners at the same time, but the prisoners could not know if the guard was watching them or not. So the prisoners had to learn to live as if the guard was watching them at every moment. As a result prisoners had to internalize the gaze of the guard because they had to assume the guard was always watching them. Bentham thought the prisoner would be reformed in the process. Foucault not so subtly called attention to Bentham's Panopticon because he thought it a metaphor for modern life.

From Foucault's perspective, the Panopticon is no less a disciplining of the body than torture. In some ways torture is less cruel because at least when you are tortured you know who has power over you. In contrast, the Panopticon is a machine in which the one whose body is subject to such an unrelenting gaze becomes the agent of his own subjection. Accordingly, the body so subjected becomes disciplined to be what the gaze of those in power desire without their power ever being made explicit.

Though our Gospel for today notes that if we do not reconcile with our brother and sister on our way to court we will end up in prison, such a reference does not seem sufficient to justify beginning with these controversial observations about modern prisons by Foucault. I have begun with Foucault, however, because I think he helps us understand why we find our texts for today anything but good news. "You have heard it said . . . but I say to you"[1] seems to make it difficult for us to join the Psalmist's celebration of how being faithful to the law is the source of our happiness.

Indeed, I think we cannot help but find a passage like our lesson from Ecclesiasticus frightening. Listen again: "For great is the wisdom of the Lord; he is mighty in power and sees everything; his eyes are on those who fear him, and he knows every human action"(15:18–19). There is no place to hide. We even say in the Confession of Sin that God knows not only those sins we have done but those sins we have committed by what we have left undone. It is as if God is in the tower in the center of the prison and we are under constant supervision.

Not only are we under a gaze we cannot escape, but our lives are back-lit by Jesus laying down demands that seem impossible to keep. Surely, we think, he has to be kidding about lust. It is enough to make you sympathetic with the Lutheran strategy to suggest this part of the Sermon on the Mount is intended to increase the awareness of our sinfulness so that we can recognize that it is only by God's grace we are saved.

There may be something to the Lutheran move, but not much. Rather, I think what is crucial is to recognize that the image of the Panopticon reflects what it means to be captured by the power of sin. The Panopticon accurately represents our presumption that we are isolated from one another and God, making it impossible for us to be of aid to one another. Isolation and imprisonment describe well not only the result of sin but the very character of sin. We are not punished for our sins, but sin is our punishment. Thus our attempt to be a law unto ourselves cannot help but make us strangers to ourselves, one another, and God.

---

1. This is a pattern throughout Matthew 5.

It is not surprising, therefore, that the god our sin creates is a moral monster who has nothing better to do than to be a voyeur who enjoys watching our failures. Such a god, a god, interestingly enough, who is the mirror image of our attempt to be our own tyrant, is as isolated as we are. Indeed, I suspect another name for such a god is Lucifer.

The God who gives us the law, however, is not a lonely watchtower God. Our God is Trinity. Our God does not exist in splendid isolation, but our God has elected from the beginning of time to have us as companions and friends. Accordingly, the law is given as a gift so that we might recognize that we are not alone. The law is not given to us as isolated individuals, but the law is given to constitute us as a people. Ecclesiasticus makes clear that we can choose to keep or not to keep the commandments, but what we cannot do is decide if there is or is not the law. We can choose to put our hand into the fire or the water, we can choose life or death, but whatever our choice the wisdom of the Lord remains. The name of that wisdom is Christ.

The church is the name of that people created by the law that is Christ. It is a people, moreover, who seem to have nothing more important to do than to argue with one another. Consider, for example, the church in Corinth. It seems Paul had begun the church but he had done so in a manner that respected that the Corinthians were yet children when it came to the Gospel. So he fed them with milk rather than solid food. Apollos followed Paul, putting before the Corinthians more solid food. The result was a divided and factional church in Corinth with some claiming to be followers of Paul and some identifying with Apollos.

Paul had no use for such divisions. He tells the Corinthians that they are not Paul's people or Apollos's people. Rather, he makes clear that they are God's people because it is God who gives them life and has enabled them to grow. Such a God is not the eternal guard of the prison, but rather the One who has come so that a people might exist in order to show the world that we are not condemned to our separate cells. That people find themselves in disagreement is not surprising given that we all remain children in God's kingdom. What is remarkable is when we are able to recognize in one another a common love of God. Such a love is necessary if we are to be a people who care enough for one another to have an argument. Love does not put an end to argument; it determines which arguments are worth having.

It is this background which better enables us to understand Jesus' "but I say to you." "But I say to you" is not back-lighting for our prison cells, but rather the key to our getting out of the prisons of our own making. We are tempted to think we can come to God and lay our gifts on the altar, as if our brother and sister do not exist. This is just between God and me. But it turns out there is no "me" isolated from my brother or sister.

Note that Jesus does not say that if I have something against my brother or sister I am to seek reconciliation. That would leave me in control. Rather, Jesus says I must go and seek reconciliation if I know that they have something against me. Reconciliation is the hard and demanding practice necessary to free us from our isolated cells of self-righteousness. To be reconciled before God is the fundamental act that makes us, the church, God's people.

Jesus does not, as Paul's admonition to the folk in Corinth exemplifies, assume that this new people he is calling into existence will be free of conflict. Followers of Christ have not ceased to be human beings. There will be disagreements and conflicts. They may wrong and hurt one another. What makes them, however, Christ's people is their refusal to leave one another alone.

They cannot leave one another alone because the God who has sought us in Christ has refused to leave us alone.

"You have heard it said . . . but I say to you" is a locution that presumes that we have more important things to do as Christians than to let lust take over our lives. It is true, moreover, the more you try to avoid lust the more attractive lust becomes. You do not will your way out of lust, or anything else. Rather, the way to overcome our temptations is to be so attracted to another way of life, a way often embodied in another you have come to love, that those temptations no longer have power over you.

Few aspects of our lives result in our isolation more than those behaviors determined by our lusts. Sin tempts us to secrecy, making impossible our ability to share our lives because we become unintelligible to ourselves. That I think is why Jesus follows his condemnation of lust by suggesting that we should not take oaths. We should not take oaths because the taking of an oath might suggest that if we had not taken the oath we might not say truthfully what we must say. To lie to ourselves or others is to betray the gift of speech. In the process of lying we lose the essential means we have been given to have lives that can be shared.

I am not unaware that some may find my framing of "You have heard it said . . . but I say to you" overly subtle. Why not just say that Jesus seems to have gone around the bend in this part of the Sermon on the Mount? We think the Beatitudes quite beautiful, but the claims that follow "but I say to you" fail to do justice to the complexity of life. Yet I think there is a profound relation between the Beatitudes and what has come to be called "the Antitheses." Just as the Beatitudes do not tell us to try to be among the mournful, but rather suggest that given Jesus' establishment of the kingdom, you should not be surprised to discover among you those who mourn. Even so, Jesus says you will discover that by becoming a disciple of Jesus your "yes" is "yes" and your "no" is "no."

Jesus' "but I say to you" is not given to imprison us, but rather it is given to free us from our self-imposed prisons. We are not isolated from one another. The exact opposite is the case. We are, using Paul's image, God's field, God's building, shaped by the common purpose to be a people determined by our worship of God. That purpose is so compelling we cannot afford to not speak plainly with one another. For we have been given the law that we might be Christ's people for the world. God has not commanded any of us to be wicked nor has he given any of us permission to sin. Rather he has given us his Christ, his law, that we might be a people capable of witnessing to the God who is with us and for us. We have been freed from the prison created by our own desires so that we might be a people capable of asking those we have wronged to forgive us.

Does that not sound like good news? We have been freed from the prison of our desires and our lies to be a people who can speak truthfully to one another. Our freedom has come from the One who was without sin; who became one of us so that we might be freed from the prison of our self-imposed isolation. Accordingly, we can share this meal as a reconciled people so that the world might know that there is an alternative to such torture. We are prisoners no more. What extraordinary good news.

7

Facing Nothingness—
Facing God

Delivered December 4, 2011

Isaiah 40:1–11
Psalm 85:1–2, 8–13
2 Peter 3:8–15a
Mark 1:1–8

In the conclusion to *The Varieties of Religious Experience* William James wrote:

> Though the scientist may individually nourish a religion and be a theist in his irresponsible hours, the days are over when it could be said that for Science herself the heavens declare the glory of God and the firmament showeth his handiwork. Our solar system, with its harmonies, is seen now as but one passing case of a certain sort of moving equilibrium in the heavens, realized by a local accident in an appalling wilderness of worlds where no life can exist. In a span of time which as a cosmic interval will count as but an hour, it will have ceased to be. The Darwinian notion of chance production, and subsequent destruction, speedy or deferred, applies to the largest as well as the smallest facts. It is impossible, in the present temper of the scientific imagination, to find in the drifting of the cosmic atoms, whether they work on the universal or

on the particular scale, anything but a kind of aimless weather, doing and undoing, achieving no proper history, and leaving no result. Nature has no one distinguishable ultimate tendency with which it is possible to feel a sympathy. In the vast rhythm of her processes, as the scientific mind now follows them, she appears to cancel herself. The bubbles on the foam which coats a stormy sea are floating episodes, made and unmade by the forces of the wind and water. Our private selves are like those bubbles—epiphenomena, as Clifford, I believe, ingeniously called them; their destinies weigh nothing and determine nothing in the world's irremediable currents of events.

In this eloquent hymn to our nothingness, James gives expression to what I suspect many fear may be the way things are. Staring into the vast darkness, the unending randomness of numberless stars, can produce in believer and non-believer alike a sense of diminishment. How dare we believe, in the face of the purposelessness of the birth and death of solar systems, including our own, that our lives count for anything. We exist but for a moment, not only as individuals but as a species. That the "weather," to use William James's language, produced for a brief time creatures conscious of their nothingness suggests that insofar as any purpose can be attributed to the process that produced such creatures, the process is best described as cruelty.

Such a view of the world is often thought to be particularly challenging for those who continue to identify with religious traditions. However, those who reject any attempt to account for our existence as determined by a god or the gods have a great difficulty justifying their commitment to the human project, given the meaninglessness of our existence. James did his best, suggesting that as long as two loving souls clung to one another in a devastated universe there would still be present real good and bad things. That position, however, has not proved persuasive for many who face the nothingness that surrounds our existence. It cannot be denied that for some the recognition that our lives finally do not matter instills in them a humility that is morally attractive. Believing that our existence makes no difference, they nonetheless try to make a difference. The universe may be hopeless, but they cannot refrain from living lives of hope. The question, of course, remains whether there is any basis for lives so lived.

At least one reason for trying to live lives that make a difference is the hope that we will not be forgotten by those who benefit from our trying to make a difference. Yet our attempts to ensure we will not be forgotten too often result in desperate manipulative strategies that are doomed to fail. Civilizations and nations come and go, families come and go, friends come and go. Such coming and going in the face of death signifies nothing. Many who live their lives in the hope of being remembered must face the reality that those they count on to remember them will also be forgotten. We may remember the Hittites (after all, they are mentioned in the Bible) but that we know a people by that name once existed does little good for them or us. Such will be our fate.

Some, faced with the sheer nothingness of our existence, draw a quite different conclusion than the humanist who thinks it important that we try to be humane. These folk, let us call them "realists," recognize that the only alternative is to kill rather than be killed. Life is a struggle. We simply must make the best of a murderous world while we can. Let tomorrow take care of tomorrow; the task is to survive the present. Those who assume such an aggressive stance can appear quite cruel, but they often do not complain when their turn comes to be killed.

They recognize that they had it coming. After all, that is the way life is.

But what about us? What about those of us gathered here to worship God with the vague hope that our lives are not pointless? Dare we acknowledge that we fear, a fear we suppress through normality, that our faith may be little more than a manifestation of our species' collective narcissism? A narcissism that cannot help but create a god or gods of our liking because we assume they exist primarily to ensure the significance of our existence. The desperate character of a faith so determined is betrayed by our inability to repress our suspicion that we live lives that seem to be no more than roles in a play written by a sadist.

The Psalmist tells us that "truth shall spring up from the earth" (Psalm 85:11). The "earthy" character of James's description of our world has the ring of truth. In the very least, we cannot help but admire James's refusal to offer false consolations or hope in the face of nothingness. There is something right, as well as ironic, about the diminishment of our existence in a world in which we have made our human existence more important than the existence of God. That is why it is surely the case that the only interesting atheism left is not the denial of God, but rather the denial by some of the significance of our existence as a human species.

William James was not a prophet. He was a philosopher whose philosophy reflected his profound humanity. Isaiah was a prophet charged by God to cry out to his people. Contrasting James and Isaiah no doubt seems like comparing apples to oranges, but the similarities and differences they represent help us see how the contrast between facing God and facing nothingness works for how we live.

Isaiah had been called by God to a specific task. He was told he was to "comfort" God's people. The Lord tells Isaiah to "speak tenderly to Jerusalem," but what Isaiah is called to "cry out" sounds anything but tender. In response to his request, "What shall I cry?" God instructs Isaiah to say to the people of Israel that "all people are grass" that withers when the breath of the Lord blows upon it. Equally important, Isaiah is to remind Israel that her constancy is like a flower that fades in the presence of the Lord (Isaiah 40:6–8).

William James would have found Isaiah's comparisons of our lives to grass and flowers a confirmation of his sense that our lives are but bubbles on the foam of a stormy sea. For Isaiah, however, this is not bad news, but rather the necessary condition for the recognition that "the word of our God will stand forever." For it turns out that the God whose word will stand forever does not exist to fulfill our fantasies that we will not have to die, either as individuals or as a species. Such a God, moreover, does not invite us to presume we can comprehend God's creation. William James, like Isaiah, may rightly remind us that our lives are not the center of the universe, but James is unable to say as Isaiah says to the people of Judah, "Here is your God!"

That God, the God of Israel, is not a God we can force to conform to our purposes. For as Isaiah makes clear, we have been created to conform to God's purposes. This, moreover, is extremely good news because it means that the world as we know it is not without purpose. It can only appear without purpose if we persist in viewing and acting in the world as if God does not exist. The question, therefore, is not does God exist, but do we? For whatever it means for us to exist, we do so as creatures created, as the universe has been created, to glorify God.

These last remarks, I fear, are properly called "metaphysical." Metaphysics, however, does not have to be, as it sometimes becomes, an esoteric philosophical discipline. Rather metaphysics is as common as our text from 2 Peter in which we are told that for the Lord one day is like a thousand years and a thousand years is like one day. That is not an invitation to try to determine the age of the earth, but rather it is a reminder that time itself is God's time. For God's time is eternity, and as God is Trinity, eternity does not mean timelessness, but rather eternity describes the reality of a time that is more than time itself.

Peter puts the matter less abstractly by addressing the question some have raised about how slowly God seems to fulfill his promises. Those who despair over God's seemingly unfulfilled promises fail to understand that the time we enjoy is but the form God's patience takes in a world that lacks patience. God's patience allows us all the time we need to be the creatures he created us to be. Again this is a reminder that to see and act in the world as God's world means that those who see the world through Jamesian eyes and those who see the world as God's world quite literally do not live in the same world.

The good news is, however, that to see the world as God's world, as God's good creation, means we have something to do. What we have to do, as Peter writes, is wait for a new heaven and a new earth. That we wait for a new heaven and earth is to learn to wait for the same One John the Baptist was called to recognize. To learn to wait for this One is to learn to live in peace with one another. To learn to live at peace with one another to be sure requires patience, but as Peter suggests we are to "regard the patience of our Lord as salvation."

Christian discipleship entails the forming of a people who know how to wait. This is Advent. This is the time of a hastening that waits. Holiness and godliness are the characteristics of a people who have faced God and by doing so have refused the nihilism that threatens all our lives in this time called modernity. To have seen the face of God in Jesus Christ gives us confidence that time is not a tale told by an idiot, but rather time names God's desire that we participate in God's very life. We are not abandoned. The heavens do declare the glory of God.

William James paid close attention to the weather, but he missed the storm that bears the name Jesus. Jesus became one of us, subject to the weather, subject to nothingness, and in the process, he redeemed time and thus gave us something to do. We have been created to be disciples of Jesus. Through baptism into this man's life, death, and resurrection, we are not fated to nothingness but rather by God's grace our fate has been transformed into a destiny otherwise unimaginable.

William James was quite right: We cannot help but appear as an accident, as purposeless as the weather in a world destined for destruction, if Jesus is not the Son of God. To view the world without God's care of us through Christ is to miss the wonder of our existence. James's description of the pointless character of our existence is indeed poetic and elegant. But it lacks the element of wonder through which God first led Israel, and now us with them, into the miracle of divine love. Once in the burning bush, now in the womb of Mary, the grandeur of creation is made manifest as God himself comes to us, reminding us who we are. We are those who receive him. This is our good work.

Christian humanism is not based on the presumption that our humanity is self-justifying. Rather, Christians are humanists because God showed up in Mary's belly. We are not an evolutionary accident. We are not bubbles on the foam that coats a stormy sea. We are God's chosen people. We have been given good work to do in a time when many no longer think there is good work. What an extraordinary claim. What extraordinary good news. Praise God, and with gratitude enjoy the glory of his creation. Together, at this time called Advent let us wait in joyful expectation for the surprising coming of the Lord.

8

Crowd Control

Palm Sunday
Delivered April 1, 2012

The Liturgy of the Palms
Mark 11:1–11

The Liturgy of the Word
Isaiah 50:4–9a
Psalm 31:9–16
Philippians 2:5–11
Mark 14:1–15:47

It is a terrible thing to fall into the hands of an admiring public. Anyone so admired cannot help but be tempted and even seduced by the terms of admiration. They may even begin to believe, in spite of the appropriate public expression of humility, that they deserve the admiration. Unable to distinguish who they are from the crowd's admiration, they soon discover they have become dependent on the expectations of their admirers. They also discover, however, that those expectations continue to increase: demands that must be met if they are to continue receiving the attention they now cannot live without. Fearing the loss of the crowd's regard, the ones so admired find themselves in a no-win game with no end in sight.

The situation is complicated further when the admiration of the crowd is aided by the many forms of what we now call "the media." Media, of course, comes in all shapes and sizes at different times and places. The admired at first cannot help but be pleased by the renown that comes from such sources. They even begin to worry if they are not being talked about, if their name is not put on a building, if they do not see their picture or name in print, they can no longer be confident they exist. Politicians who cannot resist running for something are a prime example of those who fear that loss of identity if they are out of the public eye. Yet those who become dependent on being recognized discover that those whom the media creates, the media destroys.

Palm Sunday is a wonderful celebration of the triumphal entry of Jesus into Jerusalem. Yet it is also the time that Jesus becomes subject to an admiring public. We are told "many people" spread their cloaks on the road and still others put down leafy branches to make easy the way for this king who enters Jerusalem riding on a colt. Both before Jesus and behind him people walk, shouting, "Hosanna"—a shout that signals their presumption that here is the One who has come to save Israel. They think Jesus is the long-expected king, the One who has come to restore the glory of King David's empire.

When we celebrate Palm Sunday as we do today, the liturgy invites us to take our place with the crowd that identified Jesus as their long-awaited king. Yet as we proceed through Holy Week, as we hear the accounts of Jesus' trial and crucifixion, it becomes increasingly clear that we may not have known what we were doing by joining the crowd.

Notice: There is no scriptural evidence that Jesus entered Jerusalem so that he might be praised by such a crowd. He certainly did not seem to be seduced by the crowd's admiration. That he was not seduced, I think, has everything to do with the strange juxtaposition we encounter in our texts for this morning.

Jesus is identified by the crowd as the new David, that is, the king who would restore Israel to political prominence. Yet, in the great hymn in Philippians, Jesus is described as the One who was born in our likeness, even taking the form of a slave. Humbling himself he became obedient to death, even death on the cross. In joining the crowd today, we have the advantage and disadvantage of shouting "Hosanna" alongside the tension of praising this king whom we know will soon die the death of a common criminal. We, because of the advantage of historical distance, are able to see the vulnerability of this great One who will rise to power by being raised on a cross.

The crowd that celebrated Jesus' entry into Jerusalem could not recognize the slavish nature of this king. They knew from the media of their day that kings, particularly the king to restore David's kingdom, are not slaves. Kings, moreover, are surrounded by retainers and guarded by a trained security force. Whatever the strengths and weaknesses of the disciples, they clearly would not pass muster as those set aside to consort with or protect a king. Soon, once Jesus submits to the cup set before him, the enthusiastic crowd will turn away and all his disciples will abandon him. Ironically, the only people who continue to lift him up as king are sadistic soldiers who mockingly make him a crown of thorns.

The soldiers meant their crown to be an act of derision, but this thorn-crowned king is the very One who will be "seated at the right hand of Power." He is rightly, thereby, identified by the inscription on the cross, "The King of the Jews." Yet Jesus is a king who defies what most kings assume they must do if they are to maintain power; that is, they must know how to use the admiration of the crowd to their advantage. Kings (who may bear the title of president) know they have to manipulate the crowd—maybe even use the sword—to bend the unreliable expectations of the crowd to their will. Such is the way of worldly power.

Jesus' refusal to take advantage of the crowd's enthusiasm for his own benefit indicates Jesus' power comes not from the crowd, i.e., this world, but rather from his obedience to the will of his Father. He cannot resort, therefore, to the sword or any other manipulations to ensure that he is acknowledged by the crowd. The power of this king is displayed in his willingness to glorify the Father by suffering humiliation—even to the point of death.

Are you sure you want to join the crowd? Are you sure you want to be a part of this kingdom? For the humiliation of Christ indicates the politics of his kingdom. This is clearly about power. Jesus is no less political than Caesar, but he rules not at the head of an army but from a cross. His kingship means his followers must, like him, resist being seduced by the desires and expectations of the crowd. That is why it is so important that we read the Gospel account of the crucifixion during Holy Week—Mark this year and Matthew and Luke in other years. It is the Gospel that trains us to follow Jesus not as an unruly crowd, but as disciples.

As we make our way through Holy Week, I urge you to pay particular attention to the role of the crowd. The crowd at first seems to support Jesus. We are told the chief priests and scribes even had to refrain from arresting and killing Jesus during the Passover because to do so might cause "a riot among the people." But Jesus' enemies are not deterred. The chief priests know well that crowds are subject to manipulation, and they use this knowledge to their advantage. Thus the same crowds feared by the chief priests on the day Jesus entered Jerusalem will later have Pilate release Barabbas, not Jesus. And Pilate, we are told, "wishing to satisfy the crowd," releases Barabbas. The crowd may be somewhat easy to manipulate, but even petty Roman functionaries know the crowd must be pleased.

As Americans, we pride ourselves on being individuals who defy the crowd. We think for ourselves. We believe we have the ability to make up our own minds. Yet we are quite capable of ignoring that there is no more conformist message in America than the presumption that we should each make up our minds. When you have a mind you have made up, you have become a card-carrying member of the crowd. It is sheer naiveté on our part, therefore, to think we would not have been manipulated by the chief priests. The liturgy of Holy Week won't let us get away with such self-deception; we must join the crowd in shouting, "Crucify him! Crucify him!"

That we have been given this role, moreover, is appropriate. After all, the crucifixion narratives are primarily narratives of betrayal. The crowds who will betray Jesus are only the beginning of those who will deny him. All will betray him—Judas, the disciples who cannot stay awake as he prays and who flee when he is arrested, and finally, Peter, who betrays him three times. Most chilling of all is his cry from the cross, "My God, my God, why have you forsaken me?" He is utterly abandoned, alone. This is our king.

For two thousand years, Christians have tried to make the best we could from what we can only perceive as the inadequacies of a king who would rule from a cross. We have tried to make Jesus a king acceptable to the expectations of the crowd. We have even tried to make ourselves kings who claim to rule in "his name." Jesus just did not understand the ways of the world, which means that we, who know that the crowd must be pleased, have to assume responsibility for ruling. Someone has to be king and it might as well be us.

Yet, when we try to rule in the name of the kingdom that is Christ, we lose our ability to witness to the One who emptied himself; the One who "did not regard equality with God as something to be exploited" (Philippians 2:6). Our task as followers of Christ is not to rule, but to be a people capable of witnessing to the One who rules through love, truth, and submission to the Father's will. Moreover, to follow this king and to live in his kingdom is to recognize that submission, even in the form of humiliation and suffering, leads to holiness and holiness leads to hope. This is why Christians should be a people able to negotiate the world with humor and joy, rather than fear of losing control. For it is not to the crowd that we submit, but to the One who has given us the means to resist the enticements of this world. The alternative to the crowd is the church. And the church can only be distinct from the crowd by continuously submitting to the cross of Jesus Christ.

We have been given Holy Week to train us in crowd control. Although the liturgy of this week draws us into the crowd, it does so that we might experience the tension between the crowd we join today on Palm Sunday and the crowd we will join by the end of the week. The result, hopefully, is that in the process we will recognize we are, in fact, not the crowd but the church. And while our membership in the church entails the necessary confession of our own betrayals, we submit to this training so that we may learn to sing:

Ride on, King Jesus
Ride on King Jesus, ride on.

If you want to find a way to God
The gospel highway must be trod.

Today we begin our journey with Christ along the highway that leads to his enthronement on a hill called Golgotha. May we resist the temptation to be either enamored admirers or disinterested spectators. Instead, let us follow him as faithful disciples who take this bread and this cup in humility, in obedience, and in hopeful anticipation of his glory.

9

Follow Me

Delivered October 14, 2012

Amos 5:6–7, 10–15
Psalm 90:12–17
Hebrews 4:12–16
Mark 10:17–31

Why do the disciples worry about the rich? Unlike the man who asks Jesus what he must do to inherit eternal life, the disciples, as Peter observes, have left everything to follow Jesus. The disciples clearly are not rich. As far as we can tell, Jesus and his disciples lived by begging. So why do the disciples, when they hear Jesus declare that the rich will find it difficult to enter the kingdom of God, ask him who can then be saved? Do the disciples have a mistaken understanding of salvation? But then, it is by no means clear what Jesus means by the kingdom of God.

For example, why is being rich a problem for entering the kingdom of God? Why does salvation seem to involve having (or not having) money? Jesus tells the man who asked about eternal life to give away his possessions, but he surely could not have meant that everyone must give away their wealth. If the rich gave their possessions to the poor then they would make the poor rich. We may think the rich do not have to be quite as rich as some may be, but, after all, being rich is a relative matter. We cannot help but wonder what is going on in this famous passage from the Gospel of Mark.

The prophetic denunciation of the rich by the prophet Amos seems different from the declaration by Jesus that the rich will find it difficult to enter the kingdom of God. The problem in Amos is not wealth itself, but how the rich use the power of their wealth to pervert justice. According to Amos, the rich use their money to bribe the judges who sit at the gate, resolving conflicts between people who trust them to discern what is just. Amos pronounces judgment on the rich for stealing grain from the poor, for building extravagant homes and planting vineyards, and for not even letting the poor reach the judge at the gate. He prophesies that the rich will not live to enjoy their ill-gotten gain. Again, for Amos, having wealth does not seem to be the problem, but rather how wealth perverts justice.

I suspect that, like me, you find Amos's concern for justice to be more important than questions about what salvation may or may not involve. We are ready, or at least we think we are ready, as Amos commands, to seek and love the good and hate evil. We assume to seek and love the good is equivalent to being just. Who, after all, could be against justice? Being a Christian in our day is problematic, but at least if Christians are people who care about justice, we have a chance of being identified with the good guys rather than the bad guys.

We are, therefore, more likely and willing to work for justice than we are to ask, as the rich man asks, about eternal life. We are not sure what we think about eternal life, but we are pretty sure we ought to be on the side of justice. We are sure we ought to work to make our world more just, even though, if pressed, we are not at all clear on what justice entails. For many of us, justice means voting for the left wing of the Democratic Party. The only difficulty with that strategy is that there is no left wing of the Democratic Party left.

But we persist, pursuing social strategies we think more just because we assume just social arrangements are possible, even when we are not sure if we are just. This has ecclesial implications, as religious leaders attempt to influence governments to enact laws that mandate behavior the religious leaders know they cannot expect the Christians they serve and represent to embody. For example, I was once told by a bishop that he refused a Jewish mayor's request that some of his churches offer a place for the homeless to sleep at night. The bishop reported that he told the mayor he was not going to do that because if he opened the churches, it might relieve the mayor of the responsibility of the city to care for the homeless. I suggested to the bishop that he missed the call of Jesus in the mayor's request because the mayor was reminding him of our obligation as Christians to offer hospitality. Needless to say, I am not a canon theologian of that bishop's cathedral.

Does that mean there might be some connection between justice and eternal life? In our epistle for today, we are told that the word of God is sharper than a two-edged sword, judging the thoughts and intentions of our hearts. Does justice have to do with the intentions of my heart? That strikes me as a frightening proposition, suggesting that God knows me better than I know myself. I should like to think that just to the extent I am able to hide from others, but primarily myself, the secrets of my heart also remain hidden to God. If this passage from the letter to the Hebrews suggests that this might not be the case, then it does not sound like good news to me.

But that is why I think this passage helps us understand the interaction between Jesus and this man of many possessions. For we see in their exchange what it means for the One who alone is good to look into this man's heart. The encounter between Jesus and the man asking about eternal life begins by telling us Jesus was setting out on a journey. He is confronted by this man who, with great deference, kneels before Jesus, addressing him as "Good Teacher." He seems to be a person concerned about the right thing because he asks: "What must I do to inherit eternal life?" Jesus' immediate response is to direct his attention to the One alone who is good. The One who alone is good is the same One who has given the commandments that Jesus enumerates: "You shall not murder; you shall not commit adultery; you shall not steal; you shall not be a false witness; you shall not defraud; honor your father and mother." These are the commandments the people of Israel have been given to make them a people of justice. These are the commandments Amos presupposes determines the justice rendered by judgments made by the judges at the gate.

With what seems a heartfelt response, a response that seems filled with relief, the man of many possessions confesses, "Teacher, I have kept all these since my youth." This person of great possessions has every reason to believe he is among the righteous and the just. He has always kept the law. He has done what is expected of those that appear to love the good.

But then we are told Jesus looked at him. Jesus not only looked at him, but we are told he "loved him." We dare not miss that Jesus loved him. If Jesus had not loved him, he would not have given him the great gift of the commands that seem designed specifically for this man. Jesus commanded him to do three things: (1) sell what he owned; (2) give the money to the poor; and (3) then come and follow. Each command could stand alone, but they become one by Jesus' invitation for this man to come and follow him.

That invitation, however, proved more than this man was prepared to accept because, we are told, he had great possessions. What he owned really owned him. He was the victim of the law. It seems that the law, which is perfectly just, cannot make us just. In a well-ordered society it may not be easy to discern if others (or ourselves) are what they seem. We may do everything justice demands but we cannot know if we are, in fact, just until we are confronted by the One alone who is good.

This man of great possessions, depending on your point of view, had the good or bad luck to encounter the One who alone could reveal to him where his heart lay. Is it any wonder he was shocked and went away grieving? Like most of us, he was not prepared to discover who he was. Like most of us, he did not know his life was pretense because he had not yet confronted the One who alone is good. He had not confronted Jesus. He had not confronted the One who loves us so passionately that he asks the questions necessary to expose the lies that we call "our life."

We are now, I think, in a position to understand why the disciples would ask, "Then who can be saved?" The disciples, who in the Gospel of Mark seldom understand who Jesus is or what Jesus says, at least ask the right question. Who, they wonder, can stand before this fiery furnace of love and continue to live? For this is a furnace with fire so intense it is even capable of burning away our illusions of righteousness. Confronted by such a fire is it any wonder we are hesitant to kneel before this One who is determined to overwhelm our refusal to be seen fully and yet to be loved?

Jesus' answer to the question asked by the disciples, the question we also must ask, is straightforward and unambiguous. Just as he had looked at the man of many possessions, Jesus, we are told, looked at the disciples, saying clearly that salvation cannot come from mortals, that is, from you and me. But the good news is that what is impossible for mortals is not impossible for God. For God all things are possible, making even us, frightened death-determined creatures that we are, members of the kingdom of God.

The journey that Jesus was on when confronted by the man of many possessions, we are told in Hebrews, was one that led Jesus to pass through the heavens. Jesus, the Son of God, the One who became one of us, is now with the Father and Holy Spirit, making possible our approach to the throne of God with a bold grace. We are able to do so because by assuming our flesh, but without sin, he is able to look at us with clear-eyed compassion. Jesus, the justice of God, sits at the gate judging us with the mercy of his love.

So now we know what salvation entails. Now we know what we must do to be just and to inherit eternal life—follow him.

PART III

Diverse Occasions

10

Repent

Dayspring Baptist Church
Waco, Texas
Delivered December 5, 2010

Isaiah 11:1–10
Psalm 72:1–7, 18–19
Romans 15:4–13
Matthew 3:1–12

"On that day the root of Jesse shall stand as a signal to the peoples; the nations shall inquire of him, and his dwelling shall be glorious" (Isaiah 11:10). We believe, as Paul tells us in Romans, that the day has come. The steadfast God has welcomed us Gentiles into the promises made to the patriarchs. Jesus, the root of Jesse, has come to establish his rule even over the Gentiles. Accordingly we, that is, we Gentiles, are filled with joy and peace, believing that we have been made into a people of hope through the power of the Holy Spirit.

John the Baptist came announcing that the kingdom of heaven was drawing near and that in preparation the people of Israel should repent. We believe the kingdom John announced came in the One John identified as the One whose sandals he was unworthy to carry. It turns out that Jesus didn't just bring the kingdom, but he *is* the kingdom come. Jesus, as Paul says, came as a servant to the circumcised, that is, to the people of

Israel, so that the promises to the patriarchs might be fulfilled. By doing so, Jesus brought those promises to us Gentiles, who were no people, and made us God's people. We are now storied by the promises to Israel.

Yet this is Advent. Advent is a time of waiting. But because Christians believe the promises to the patriarchs have been fulfilled in Jesus Christ, we are not sure what it means for us to wait. Jews, who do not recognize our Christ as the fulfillment of the promises to Abraham, are a people in waiting. We Christians believe the kingdom has come, which means we are not at all sure we know what it means for us to wait.

Because we are not quite sure what it means for us to wait, it is not clear we know how to read Isaiah 11. We love the image of the kingdom depicted in the passage. The wolf now lives with the lamb, the leopard sleeps with the kid, the calf and the lion are led by a little child, the cow and the bear graze in the same field, and the nursing child plays over the hole of the asp. These strong and beautiful images capture our imagination. In particular they captured the imagination of the Quaker Edward Hicks, whose depictions of the peaceable kingdom many of us have come to love. I have even written a book titled *The Peaceable Kingdom*.

But there is a small problem, a problem that Nietzsche saw quite clearly; that is, wolves are quite happy to have lambs lie down with them. Lambs are quite tasty. In a similar fashion, Jeff Stout, in his book *Blessed are the Organized: Grassroots Democracy in America*, observes that some churches are "so enraptured by utopian visions of lions lying down with the lamb that they are unwittingly assisting actual lions in the destruction of actual lambs." It may be, Stout suggests, that utopian visions have an uplifting role to play but they become dangerous when they interfere with legitimate attempts to constrain what lions are presently doing to lambs.

That Stout, like many, has confused wolves with lions does not make his argument any less pressing. Let us confess we are not quite sure what to say in response to a Nietzsche or Stout. We believe that Jesus is the root of Jesse. Isaiah tells us, "On that day the root of Jesse shall stand as a signal to the peoples," but that day, a day when the alienation of our lives from God, our neighbor, and ourselves has ended, does not seem to have arrived. You can talk all you want about the delay of the kingdom, you can play the already against the not-yet, but the images of the peaceable kingdom are too strong and they tempt us to force the kingdom into existence. This temptation is fueled by our fear that we have no answer to the taunt, "If Jesus is who you say he is, why do lambs continue to be eaten by wolves?"

A troubling challenge, particularly if you are, like me, a pacifist. I am a pacifist because I believe that Jesus is the root of Jesse. I am a pacifist because I believe that through the cross God has established his nonviolent kingdom of love. But if the vision of Isaiah 11 is but utopian fantasy, a commitment to nonviolence can rightly be dismissed as a position of the privileged whose lives depend on the safety secured by wolves. If that is true, where is the good news in that?

The good news is Advent. The good news is that because Jesus is the root of Jesse we have all the time in the world to be at peace with one another and all of God's creation. Advent is the time constituted by the inclusion of us Gentiles into the promises to the patriarchs so that all might know that the God who created us for God's enjoyment refuses to save us by forcing us to live at peace with one another. To learn to so live is to learn to wait in patience.

Advent, moreover, is a time of repentance because repentance is the transformation necessary to produce people of a new age who have not lost their connection to Israel. For if we lose our connection to Israel, we lose our connection to Christ who is the root of Jesse. The kingdom now present in Christ is the kingdom constituted by our being made a new people through such a repentance.

Let us confess, however, that we are not sure why repentance is important or even what it might look like. Most of us are willing, like the Pharisees and Sadducees, to fake it because we have been told we need to repent. But faking repentance becomes an exercise in narcissism in pietistic drag. For example, consider John Howard Yoder's reflections on how repentance is often understood:

> Protestantism, and perhaps especially evangelical Protestanism, in its concern for helping every individual to make their own authentic choice in full awareness and sincerity, is in constant danger of confusing the kingdom itself with the benefits of the kingdom. If anyone repents, if anyone turns around to follow Jesus in this new way of life, this will do something for the aimlessness of their life. It will do something for their loneliness by giving them fellowship. It will do something for their anxiety and guilt by giving them a good conscience. So the Bultmanns and the Grahams whose "evangelism" is to proclaim the offer of restored selfhood, liberation from anxiety and guilt, are not wrong. If anyone repents, it will do something for their intellectual confusion, by giving them doctrinal meat to digest, a heritage to appreciate, and a conscience about telling it all as it is: So "evangelicalism" with its concern for hallowed truth and

reasoned communication is not wrong; it is right. If a person repents it will do something for their moral weakness by giving them the focus for wholesome self-discipline, it will keep them from immorality and get them to work on time. So the Peales and the Robertses who promise that God cares about helping me squeeze through the tight spots of life are not wrong; they have their place. BUT ALL OF THIS IS NOT THE GOSPEL. This is just the bonus, the wrapping paper thrown in when you buy the meat, the "everything" which will be added, without taking thought for it, if we seek the kingdom of God and his righteousness.[1]

"BUT ALL OF THIS IS NOT THE GOSPEL"? Yoder surely cannot be serious. Most of the sermons we hear presuppose that the Gospel is about our lives having a purpose or meaning. Is not the Gospel about forgiveness of sin, which results in our ability to have a good, or at least a less troubled, conscience? Or in a more existential vein, isn't the Gospel about liberation from death-induced anxiety that tempts us to overwhelming pride or the sloth of despair? Does not our salvation require, moreover, the holding of right beliefs about God and God's relation to creation? How can Yoder, a pacifist, even begin to suggest the Gospel does not entail living a morally upright life? Yet Yoder claims that all these results, results that are no doubt significant, are not the Gospel.

According to Yoder the good news of God's revolution is not that violence is only wrong when the bad guys use it. Nor does the good news mean that the only way to live nonviolently

---

1. John Howard Yoder, *The Original Revolution: Essays on Christian Pacifism* (Scottsdale, PA: Herald Press, 2003).

entails fleeing to the desert. Nor does it involve the inner-worldly emigration of the Pharisees to refuse cooperation with the powers only at the point of personal complicity. Also rejected is the strategy of the Sadducees, that is, the attempt to get enough good people willing to work within the system in the hope that some good or at least a lesser evil can result.

No, the good news, the Gospel, is that through the cross and resurrection a people of patience have been called into existence, a people who have the time, in an impatient world of violence, to welcome one another. According to Paul, we are able to welcome one another because we have been welcomed by Christ. And this welcome is not "I am so glad to see you," but rather "my life depends on your life." And so this welcome entails a patient waiting on one another, because no one can be forced to accept Christ's invitation to become a part of the people of God. Any invitation marked by force rather than patient waiting cannot be the same invitation extended to us in Christ.

A people who have learned to wait, therefore, are filled with a joy-determined peace because the life they have been given is so wonderfully interesting. They are freed from the boredom that too often is the breeding ground of violence. Repentance is the name given to the transformation through baptism by which we are made a people of hope in a world without hope. To repent is to remember one's baptism—it is to remember that Christ is our hope and the hope of the world. A people so constituted cannot expect to be celebrated. They may even be ridiculed, they may even be persecuted, they may even be identified as Jewish, but they fear not the judgment of the world. Rather they delight, as Isaiah suggests, in the fear of the Lord.

It is true we live in a world of wolves and that it is not safe to be a lamb. If Jesus is the root of Jesse, what are we to make of the predatory character of animals (and, for that matter, of life)? I think this: God has refused to coerce any of God's creation, a world of wolves and lambs, to live at peace because peace cannot be coerced. The peaceable kingdom envisioned in Isaiah 11 is one that must be inhabited. Those of us who have been baptized into Christ inhabit that kingdom because he is the kingdom. The degree to which we will see the wonderful images of that kingdom where the wolves and lambs exist peacefully alongside one another surely begins with us, that is, those baptized into the life and death of Jesus. It begins with our refusing to kill one another. Let the wolves imitate us as we imitate Christ.

We can refuse to kill because the Father has accepted the Son's sacrifice so that the promise to Israel may be extended to the Gentiles. That is the good news. That is the Gospel. The peaceable kingdom has come, making possible a people who have learned to wait because they trust in a God who refuses to coerce anyone into the love that is God's life. This is Advent— God's time, a time constituted by repentance, a time of peace. So let us rejoice and be glad that we have been made heirs of God's promises to the patriarchs.

11

Coming Home

Pleasant Mound–Urban Park United Methodist Church
Pleasant Mound, Texas
Delivered October 16, 2011

Exodus 33:12–23
Psalm 99
1 Thessalonians 1:1–10
Matthew 22:15–22

This sanctuary was finished. The congregation of Pleasant Mound Methodist Church soon gathered on a Sunday to celebrate that wonderful accomplishment. At that event my father, who had served as the general superintendent for the construction of the church, was appropriately thanked and honored for his good work. My father, a modest man not accustomed to being in the public eye, responded by observing: "I would like to say I am only human. The One we should be thanking is Almighty God. He is the One that gave it to us. Words will not let me express myself."

I begin with my father's words, words that indeed did express my father's faith, to remind us that it remains true that what we are here to do is to thank and praise God for the gifts he has given us. I do so because I am aware that this is a special occasion for me and for you. You have graciously invited me to come home in order to celebrate my life and my work. That you

78

are willing to claim me is a gift I am sure I do not deserve, but I will nonetheless gratefully accept.

Of course it may be that your embrace of me is also a way to celebrate this part of Dallas called Pleasant Grove. I have been told that Pleasant Grove has acquired a reputation since I left. Pleasant Grove may have had a similar reputation when I lived here, but I was not sufficiently aware to have recognized it did so. All I knew was it mattered who won the football game on Friday night.

The reputation that the Grove seems to have acquired, I suspect, was embodied in a remark made to me by a Dallas old-timer. Learning I was from Pleasant Grove, he observed that I defied the odds because most people raised in Pleasant Grove are not able to leave Pleasant Grove. He seemed to suggest that I gave lie to the presumption that no good can come from "the Grove." So let me say as straightforwardly as I can: I am happy to be identified with the hard-working people of Pleasant Grove, Texas. This is my home.

That you take pride in my "accomplishments," however, means you are very strange people. I am a theologian. Theologians are not usually counted among the successful in our society. For most people it is not even clear what it is that theologians do. But you are the church. You think it important that theologians exist. You even think they should be celebrated. I was taught that you should never look a gift horse in the mouth. I am certainly not going to examine your teeth. I assume you must have known what you were doing when you invited me to come home.

I am profoundly grateful to you for your hospitality and for making this an unforgettable event. So I hope that you will not think me ungrateful for what you have done if I say, "I am only human. The One we should be thanking is Almighty God. He is the One that gave it to us." We are, after all, here to worship God.

God, not my or your accomplishments, is what we celebrate on this day. We are here to thank and praise God for our creation and redemption. Whatever we have done that deserves recognition can only be acknowledged if what we have done is but a reflection of God's glory.

So on this homecoming it is particularly important for me to remember that we are here to worship God. Homecomings are occasions fraught with temptations, not the least being a romanticizing of the past. The title of Thomas Wolfe's great novel *You Can't Go Home Again* is an important reminder that we cannot help but be a stranger to our past. I am not the same person who some fifty years ago preached his first horrible sermon from this pulpit, nor are you the same people who had to hear that moralistic exercise of self-righteous arrogance. Likewise, it is good to celebrate the faithfulness of Pleasant Mound United Methodist Church, but we dare not forget that this was a church so inured in the habits of the time, many of us did not even know we were segregated.

But this is Pleasant Grove. The very fact that this is Pleasant Grove means we have the reality of this place to call into question any temptation we might have to idealize the past. Rather, what we can do is praise God for making us a people who are capable of change. Most of you are not the people who instilled in me the first glimmerings of faith in God, but you can thank God that such people existed to make possible my faith and your faith. Paul wrote to the Thessalonians saying that everywhere he goes there is no need to speak of the faith of the Thessalonians because their faith had become known in distant places. In like manner, there is no need to try to whitewash the past because by your very existence in this church at this time we know God found the lives of those who worshiped here sufficient to sustain us as God's church.

Another temptation associated with homecoming, particularly a homecoming like this one, is for the one who has come home to think they deserve the praise they are receiving. Of course we can try to play at being humble, but that is exactly what we do, namely, we play at being humble. It turns out it is a contradiction to think we can try to be humble. Humility is a virtue that rides on the back of lives that have been given such good work it never occurs to them to credit what they do as an accomplishment.

Moses understood this. In the Old Testament lesson for today, Moses has an interesting conversation with the Lord. The Lord has instructed Moses to "Bring up this people" (Exodus 33:12), and to assure him that this would be possible, the Lord reminds Moses that he has found favor in his sight. It would seem that having been favored by God would be more than enough assurance. Indeed, most fragile egos, tempted by the lure of entitlement, would take this and run, ruling it over others. If ever there were something to boast about, it would be having been favored by the Lord. But Moses did not take it and run. Rather, he "stayed put" and asked for more. In particular, he asked that the Lord remain with him and show him his ways. Why? Moses says, "so that I may know you" (Exodus 13:13). Moses took little comfort in being favored by God; he wanted to know God. Perhaps he knew himself well enough to know that he would be tempted to think too highly of himself if being favored became the defining characteristic of his relationship with God and God's people. Rather than allowing such self-deceit, Moses understood that the true gift is in basking in God's glory—not our own. The true gift is the Lord himself.

In our Gospel lesson for today, the disciples of the Pharisees and the Herodians approach Jesus with a new strategy to try to show he is not a faithful Jew. They try to flatter him. "Teacher, we know that you are sincere, and teach the way of God in accordance with the truth, and show deference to no one, for you do not regard people partially." They hope their flattery will allow them to catch Jesus off-guard when they ask what appears to be a harmless question, "Tell us, is it lawful to pay taxes to the emperor, or not?" The question is designed to trap Jesus by forcing him to choose between loyalty to the God of Israel or to Rome. In short, they are trying to make him acknowledge that, given Rome's power in Palestine, the worship of God cannot command every aspect of life. Political realism requires that the emperor's power be acknowledged.

Jesus is, so to speak, on to them. He has no time for such trickery. His use of the coin does not suggest he thinks Caesar has any claim on the coins bearing Caesar's image, but rather he asks to see the coins because even to carry a coin with the image of Caesar on it betrays Jewish existence. That his questioners possess the coins indicates they are flirting with an idolatrous practice. They are already under the spell of the emperor. Jesus' suggestion that they are to give to the emperor what is the emperor's is filled with irony. They clearly have already sided with the emperor.

Jesus is, therefore, not suggesting that the emperor has claim on anything. Rather it is Jesus' way to make clear that there is nothing that God does not possess, including the life and image of the emperor. The emperor wants it all but so does God. This is a zero-sum game. You cannot worship God and mammon, or the emperor. You cannot be loyal in some things to God and in other things to the emperor.

Those who questioned Jesus about paying taxes to the emperor assumed that they were free of idolatry. Jesus' question

about the coin revealed that his questioners were already impli-
cated in an idolatrous way of life. The deep problem with idolatry is our presumption that we would know it when we see it.
But idolatry is a subtle sin; it hides from us our implicit ways
of life that give lie to our worship of God. That is particularly
the case in social orders like our own when we are encouraged to
become our own tyrants.

Commentators on this brief but extremely important
exchange between Jesus and the Pharisees and the Herodians
seldom notice the relation between flattery and idolatry in this
passage. The disciples of the Pharisees and the Herodians first
approach Jesus using flattery. They know that those in power
love to be flattered. Those in power love to be flattered because
they know how pretentious their claim to power is. They need
flattery to legitimize their claims to deserve the status they enjoy.
In the process, they, as well as those who flatter them, come to
believe their own press releases. They idolize their own lives
because they believe who they are and what they have done is
not a gift but an accomplishment.

If I am able to avoid believing my own press releases it
is because God gave me a father who would say at a decisive
moment in his life, "I would like to say I am only human. The
One we should be thanking is Almighty God. He is the One that
gave it to us." To have such a father is to be given a gift that forces
recognition that all life is a gift. No one deserves having such a
father, but then none of us deserve life itself. That is why we are
here to worship God. We are here to worship God because God
has given us life itself.

The question for me, therefore, is not: How did I get from
Pleasant Grove to Duke University? The question is not: How
did I become a success? Whatever it might mean for a theologian

to be a success. The question is: How have I been so fortunate to have people in my life to remind and force me to recognize that this is not about me? This is about God. It is about the God that I am sure was present at Pleasant Mound United Methodist Church when I was growing up. A church that, like all churches, was often less than it should have been, but that did not prevent God from showing up—even in Pleasant Grove.

That same God, I am sure, is present in the ministry of Annelda Crawford. That same God, I am sure, is present in you—a people capable of recognizing and resisting the idolatries that tempt us to live lives in which God is but an afterthought. I say this not to flatter you, but rather I say this because I know the gift of Jesus Christ has set you free.

That is why I can only thank you, a people who know that what we do at this time and in this place is thank God in order that we might reflect his glory. Amen.

12

Transfigured

Church of the Redeemer
Sarasota, Florida
Delivered March 6, 2011

Exodus 24:12–18
Psalm 2
2 Peter 1:16–21
Matthew 17:1–9

Peter Storey, the former Methodist bishop and president of the South African Council of Churches, a white man who opposed apartheid, tells a story about a party at which he and Archbishop Desmond Tutu were the honored guests. It was hosted by black South Africans who had leadership positions in their post-apartheid society. They asked Peter and Desmond Tutu if they understood why they were throwing this party for them. They replied: "Because we were with you in the days of struggle against apartheid." Their hosts responded by saying, "No, because you baptized us; you told us who we were and remembered when no one else did."

I begin with this story, a story that at once connects baptism and politics, because I think it is a story that helps us move from Epiphany to Lent. Lent began as the time for catechumens to undergo the strict discipline of fasting and repentance in preparation for their baptism at the Pascha. In the fourth century, with the end of persecution and the lowering of standards for the many who would now be Christians, it became customary for the faithful to join the catechumens in their pre-baptismal fast. All Christians were also encouraged to attend to instruction in Christian doctrine as part of their renewal.

Of course doctrine could not and was not separated from disciplines of prayer and fasting. The interdependence of prayer and doctrine was forged during this time by the development of an innovative way of life called monasticism. I think it not accidental that at the same time that Christianity became the legal religion of the Roman Empire, some Christians took on a way of life that suggested that the worship of Christ would always be a challenge to the status quo. The monks became the church's imagination to help the church remember what it means to be a people of repentance.

Lent was not just another exercise for the devout, rather it was an obligation incumbent on every Christian. Of course those who wished could continue to pray and fast with fervor at other seasons, but the observance of Lent meant that the sanctity of the church as a whole was at stake. So Lent was intended to be a corporate effort by the whole church to live, at least for a season, as befitted the body of Christ. Through fervent and frequent prayer and in a serious and mortified spirit, a corporate Easter communion was made possible in which all might celebrate as members of the body of Christ.

But what does the transfiguration have to do with the transition from Epiphany to Lent? And what does baptism, as the story with which I began seems to suggest, have to do with helping a people sustain a struggle against oppression? Let me begin to try to answer those questions by observing that the transfiguration is a baptismal event. The transfiguration recalls Jesus' baptism by John and, in doing so, becomes a way to prepare the disciples for their baptisms by the Holy Spirit. That baptism, that is, the baptism of the disciples into Jesus' death and resurrection, is necessary to create and sustain a people of a new age.

A people transfigured by such a baptism, a people who have been told whose they are, cannot help but be an alternative to the politics of the world. The politics of the world is a politics that depends, as Peter suggests, on "cleverly devised myths" that inevitably promise more than they can deliver. Such myths are necessary because a worldly politics cannot acknowledge that the Lord, that is, the king named in our psalm for today, is the crucified Jesus. Only a people so transfigured, a people who have through baptism "stared down death," can sustain the long, arduous struggle against injustice.

I suspect you rightly are thinking, "What did he just say?" Paula, my good wife, a United Methodist minister appointed by her bishop to an ecumenical ministry at the Episcopal Church of the Holy Family, has the task of reading my sermons in the hope of making them coherent. She often observes that my sermons are "tight." An accurate description, I suspect, but one for which I am not about to apologize. Rather, let me try to make explicit the connections between the transfiguration, baptism, and politics asserted in the previous paragraph. By making those connections, I hope to show that nothing is more important for our lives than to see how our baptism into the death and resurrection of Jesus can free us from the ever-present myths that threaten to destroy our lives.

When Jesus was baptized by John, we are told that the Spirit of God descended like a dove and rested on him. A voice from heaven then said, "This is my Son, the Beloved, with whom I am well pleased" (Matthew 17:5). At the transfiguration, Jesus' face shone like the sun and his clothes became dazzling white, and from the cloud that overshadowed Jesus, Moses, and Elijah came a voice saying, "This is my Son, the Beloved; with him I am well pleased; listen to him." The transfiguration is the confirmation of John's baptism of Jesus and only now we begin to understand what that means. For the transfiguration follows Peter's confession and Jesus' rebuke of Peter for failing to understand that Jesus is to be killed only to be raised on the third day. The glory that surrounds him on the mountain is the glory that comes from the Father in recognition of the perfect obedience of Jesus so that the law and the prophets may be fulfilled. That is why the presence of Moses and Elijah is so important.

But it is equally important that we not miss the apocalyptic character of the transfiguration. Jesus has just told his disciples that the Son of Man is to come and that some now present will not see death before his arrival. Accordingly, the transfiguration of Jesus means the die is cast, confirming that the Son of Man has come. But his death by crucifixion and his subsequent resurrection is still to come. Thus he ordered Peter, James, and John that they were to "tell no one about the vision until after the Son of Man has been raised from the dead" (Matthew 17:9). The disciples are sworn to silence because they are not yet ready to be witnesses to the One transfigured by the cross. They are not ready because they have not yet undergone the training necessary to acknowledge that the One long expected does not conquer on the world's terms. The glory they have witnessed on the mountain might tempt them to presume that all has been accomplished at the transfiguration. Peter even suggests that they build booths in which they might dwell. The disciples do not yet understand that the glory they have witnessed on the mountain is the glory of the One whose obedience culminates in the cross. For Jesus is the One who will defeat the kingdoms of death by exposing those kingdoms for what they are, that is, false dominions whose pretensions, as our Psalmist suggests, God holds in derision.

In the letter from Peter we read today, I think we have a clear indication that Peter had learned what it means to be witness to the glory of the crucified One. It seems his letter is in response to some in the church who think they know when Jesus will return while others wonder if he is ever to return. From Peter's perspective, both groups are following schemes of their own devising making Jesus a savior determined by their fantasies about what a savior is to do. But Peter has witnessed the glory of the Lord at the transfiguration. He has heard the voice, a voice of Majestic Glory, saying "This is my Son, my Beloved, with whom I am well pleased" (Matthew 17:5). Peter, as the voice commands, has "listen[ed] to him." He has followed him, even as he had betrayed him, to the cross. Peter is not tempted, therefore, to engage in speculation shaped by cleverly devised myths about when Jesus will come again or, given that some think he will never return, how to run the world.

Rather, Peter has learned all he needs to know to be a follower of the One who rules the world by conquering death. What Peter knows is that through the cross and resurrection of Jesus, the powers of oppression and injustice have been defeated. The task for those who would follow Jesus is to live according to that reality. The powers of this age have been defeated. We do them no favor if we act in a manner that affirms their delusion that they are in control. Rather we should imitate God, who our psalm describes as laughing at those who think they are in control. The Son of Man has returned, restoring God's rule and thus humbling kings who would rule as if there is no God.

I fear we, who never think of ourselves as kings but believe nonetheless that we rule ourselves and the world, are among those who should be so humbled. We live refusing to believe the Son of Man has come. We are pretty sure, if we are to get out of life alive, we are going to have do what we fear God failed to do when he set Jesus on the road to Jerusalem. Cross and resurrection are all well and good, but someone has to do the things that need to be done to make history come out right. Thus the cleverly devised myth that America is the hope of the world—a myth that we allow to give us the false confidence that we know who we are, we know where we are, and we know how to get to where we want to go.

But Lent beckons. Again we are forced to contemplate repentance. We have not lived as those who believe that the Son of Man has come. We are desperate to be in control of our lives in a world in which we are not in control. We are possessed by cleverly devised myths that are so constitutive of our lives we are unable to acknowledge their power over us. We do not live, we cannot imagine what it would mean to live, as if the Son of Man has come transfigured and thus transfigures our lives so that we might glow in the glory of the Lord. But if we do not reflect the glory of the One transfigured, then the world has no light to see that all is not darkness.

The good news, however, is that we have been baptized. It is not by accident that the newly-baptized in the ancient church were clothed in white as they emerged from that transfiguring bath. They understood that they had been transformed through baptism. No longer would they be subject to the powers fueled by our fear of death. A free people has been born through baptism into the death and resurrection of this, the Son of Man. We have been shown who we are.

So let us rejoice as we are drawn from the transfiguration toward Ash Wednesday and into Lent. Let us remember our baptisms. Let us be renewed through that remembrance so that we might be shown once again who we are by the One who has created us. For our baptism has been made possible by the transfiguration of Jesus, prefiguring, as that event did, his resurrection. Through baptism we are re-membered into the body of Christ, and so re-membered we discover we have all the time in the world to be God's people for the world. Such a people can strive for justice without being tempted to use means that too often imitate the means of those who would oppress us. So let us repent, remember our baptisms, and hope that our lives might reflect the glory that is Christ.

13

Recognizing Jesus/ Seeing Salvation

Duke Divinity School
Feast of the Presentation
Delivered February 2, 2012

Malachi 3:1–4
Psalm 24:7–10
Hebrews 2:14–18
Luke 2:22–40

It is quite embarrassing. They just did not seem to "get it." Perhaps it was because they were old. The old often fail to pick up—or maybe just ignore—the cultural cues those more attuned to the spirit of the age use to trigger the socially-appropriate response to situations in which they find themselves. Or it may be because they were, how to put it delicately, so religious they failed to understand what the occasion required. I suppose we cannot help but think lives that have been spent waiting for the Messiah will not be exactly normal. Simeon does not sound like someone capable of delightful conversation. Anna may even be less scintillating than Simeon. Do you really want to know someone who, after the early death of her husband, has spent her life fasting and praying night and day in the temple?

Just think about it. If you had been in the temple when Mary and Joseph came with the baby Jesus, you would have known what to say. Like me, you would have blurted out, "What a cute baby!" Of course, we inhabit a very different culture and time than Mary, Joseph, Simeon, and Anna, but I cannot help but believe that even in Palestine, even in a country occupied by the Romans, there would have been an equivalent response to our "What a cute baby!" After all, we are human beings and human beings, even though we live in different times and in diverse cultures, seem to share the judgment that most babies are cute. So how are we to account for Simeon and Anna's failure to respond to this baby as we would expect? Why do they, ignoring all suggestion of cultural convention, see this baby Jesus as God's long-awaited salvation for Israel?

I am, of course, having fun. But I begin this way to help us recognize how extraordinary it was that Simeon and Anna see that this baby is God's salvation. What makes it possible to see salvation carried in the arms of Mary? Most of us would see a baby, but Simeon and Anna, guided by the Holy Spirit, saw this baby named Jesus to be the long-awaited savior of Israel who would even be a light of revelation to the Gentiles. What made it possible for Simeon and Anna to so see Jesus?

Rather than keep you in suspense, let me tell you what I take to be the difference between us, that is, those of us who would have just seen a baby, and Simeon and Anna, who saw salvation. The difference is found in what Simeon says will happen through this baby; that is, the glory of Israel will go as a light for revelation to the Gentiles. What is Israel's glory? Israel's glory is being God's chosen people, a people who have been given the gifts of the law and the prophets in order to live as a holy people. Israel knows she has often betrayed God's gifts, but Israel nonetheless is steadfast in her conviction that God's salvation can be seen—perhaps preeminently seen—in the sacrifices enacted in the temple.

We are Gentiles. To be sure, we are Christian Gentiles, but we are not sure what to make of Israel's presumption that salvation can be seen. We are tempted to think of salvation in terms of generalized ideals we think all humanity shares (or should share) rather than a salvation that is seen in the glory of Israel. We are not at all sure, therefore, we can or should be able to see salvation, which means, I fear, we can no longer see Jesus as Simeon and Anna did.

In some liturgical calendars the Feast of the Presentation brings an end to the season of Christmas. I suspect no season of the Christian year threatens to drown the Gospel in sentimentality more than Christmas. This sentimentality, moreover, is often the result of our desire to have Jesus without the Jews. As Christians, we are tempted to think of Christmas as "the beginning" of the story; it is all too easy to forget that our celebration of Christ's birth entails the claim that this child is the very One whom the Jews had long been waiting for. Indeed, the proclamations of Simeon and Anna reaffirm and fulfill the prophecies that mark our Advent season of waiting and preparation. The long-awaited salvation of Israel—and with it our own salvation—is here, present in this child.

But salvation will come at a cost. The polarities of life and death mark each birth, and this child is no different. If anything, death, even agonizing death, lingers around this child. Simeon's aside to Mary indicates he is keenly aware of this. Thus, it is hardly a coincidence that the overarching context for today's Gospel lesson is the sacrificial act of purification. From Malachi, we read that God, being displeased with the lack of righteousness among his people, will be sending a messenger who, like a refiner's fire, will "purify the descendants of Levi" so that they might "present offerings to the Lord in righteousness." The litany of Psalm 24 asks, "Who shall ascend the hill of the Lord? And who shall stand in his holy place?" And the response comes back, "Those who have clean hands and pure hearts, who do not lift up their souls to what is false, and do not swear deceitfully. They will receive blessing from the Lord, and vindication from the God of their salvation."

Perhaps it is helpful to imagine the Presentation as a scene not unlike the scenes we witness at infant baptisms. We tend to think the babies cry because of the ineptness of the minister or the temperature of the water. Yet it may well be that they are angered by what we do to them. Through baptism, they are being subjected to a death. To be sure, it is a death that we believe gives life, but nonetheless what they have undergone is a fearful business. The Presentation of Christ in the temple is no less fearful.

Luke is intent on reminding us that the purification of Mary and Jesus is required by a law that reflects a history of life and death. In Exodus 13, the Lord tells Moses that "every firstborn male shall be designated as holy to the Lord." And in preparation for future generations he is instructed, "When in the future your child asks you, 'What does this mean?' you shall answer, 'By strength of hand the Lord brought us out of Egypt, from the house of slavery. When Pharaoh stubbornly refused to let us go, the Lord killed all the firstborn in the Land of Egypt, from human firstborn to the firstborn of animals. Therefore I sacrifice to the Lord every male that first opens the womb, but every firstborn of my sons I redeem." This sacrificial act, therefore, is a reminder of the Lord's mercy—his redemption of Israel from her Egyptian oppressors.

Thus Mary presents herself with her son in the temple at Jerusalem forty days after his birth so she and he may be purified as the law demands. The temple is where the priests of Israel

(Simeon may even have been a priest) enact the sacrifices that God desires both for the purification of sin and for the remembrance of God's mercy to his people.

Being too poor to afford a lamb, Joseph and Mary sacrifice a pair of turtledoves and two young pigeons. In doing so, they recognize the Lord's mercy in accepting the sacrifice of these animals rather than the sacrifice of their firstborn son. While this particular act was not exceptional on the part of Mary and Joseph—they were, after all, simply being faithful to the law— this narrative of the Presentation is a foreshadowing of the eventual self-sacrifice Jesus will perform on the cross. In this initial sacrificial process, Jesus is consecrated to be for Israel—and for us—the great high priest, the Lamb of God, who will sacrifice himself so that we, Jew and Gentile, might become a light to the nations. We are told in Hebrews he did not come to help angels, but rather he came to the descendants of Abraham, becoming in every respect like his brothers and sisters so that he might "be a merciful and faithful high priest in the service of God, to make a sacrifice of atonement for the sins of the people." The Presentation is the first step on the pathway to atonement.

Simeon and Anna are able to recognize who this baby is because their vision has been disciplined by faithful observance of Israel's sacrificial life centered on the temple. That Simeon and Anna expect to see Israel's salvation makes those of us who are Christians distinctly uncomfortable. The challenge, "If Jesus has brought salvation, why does the world seem like it is all going to hell in a hand basket?" stings because we can't deny the truthfulness of the observation that the state of the world hardly seems to validate our confession that salvation has come. We are even tempted to deny that it has, instead fixating on Christ's coming again. We prefer to defer recognition by assuming we will see

salvation when all has been judged and made right in the escha-
ton. But that is hardly the good news of the Gospel! If we refuse
to see salvation now, how can we expect to recognize it then?
The question for us today is: Have we been disciplined enough
by the sacramental life of the church to recognize Jesus when he
is in our midst?

Simeon and Anna, schooled by the work of the Holy Spirit,
are able to see that salvation is this baby who, as we are told in
Hebrews, shares our flesh, our dying, so that the power of death
might be destroyed, freeing us from the fear of death. But their
joyful proclamations do not invite a naïve belief that salvation
has put an end to conflict and struggle. For the God who saves
by becoming one of us is the God who refuses to indulge our
illusions that peace is won through control, manipulation, and
violence. Rather, God comes to us as a baby, vulnerable and sus-
ceptible to the world's fearsome grasp for power. That he does
so means our fantasies of control will be exposed, our inner
thoughts revealed. Herein is the conflict and struggle of working out our salvation. To recognize salvation in this child means
admitting to ourselves that this is not the kind of salvation we
desire. To see salvation requires eyes trained to see sin so that
when we present ourselves in the temple—before God and
neighbor—we might do so with clean hands and pure hearts.
This is why the prayer of confession rightly comes before the
eucharistic celebration. The One whom we receive through the
holy sacraments is the very One who, through the power of the
Holy Spirit, cleanses us of sin so that we might behold him in
his glory.

The story of Christ's Presentation and Simeon's and Anna's
recognition is one we believe to be reenacted through us today.
For it is the same Holy Spirit that led Simeon to take the

Christ-child in his arms and proclaim "my eyes have seen your salvation!" (Luke 2:30) that leads us to take up the cup of salvation and bear witness to his sacrifice for us.

Therefore, sisters and brothers, let us confess our sins and ascend the hill of the Lord. For it is on the hill that we have seen our salvation—and the salvation of the world. Let us present ourselves to the Lord, who in these sacraments presents himself to us once again. And by his mercy, in receiving these gifts, may we become one so that in us the world might see salvation.

14

Trust

A Sermon for Founder's Day at Duke University
Duke University Chapel
Delivered September 30, 2012

Esther 7:1–6, 9–10; 9:20–22
Psalm 124
James 5:13–20
Mark 9:38–50

We are born into webs of trust so thick and near to us we can and do miss their significance for our very survival. The child cannot help but unconditionally trust others if he or she is to survive. Trust may be justified or explained in some of its forms as a self-interested strategy. Yet trust, the trust we rely on for life itself, the trust we should like to have in ourselves, is so basic, so primitive, we cannot attribute it entirely to self-interest. Trust, it seems, at the most basic level entails an unavoidable, primordial openness to others.

Yet it is also true that we are born into webs of mistrust that threaten our survival. We cannot help but look away from the eyes of the orphan who has never been held. What horror could be more frightening than the child who has never experienced the trust of touch? Never touched, these children become incapable of touching. We cannot help but ask, "Are these children human?" No betrayal is more basic than the child so isolated that he or she is made incapable of the love trust makes possible.

Trust is like the air we breathe. We fail to notice that trust constitutes our lives until we sense its perversion or absence. Trust, for example, is essential to conversation because by speech we hand ourselves over to another in the hope of receiving from them a response. This is true even in an exchange with a stranger. We trust a stranger's words unless he or she has given us reason not to trust them. We are determined to trust one another for if we did not we would be unable to get on with life. We are fated to trust and to be trusted.

The depth of emotion we feel when we have been betrayed is an indication of how deeply our lives depend on trust. We have to trust one another, but the trust that makes our lives possible also makes us vulnerable. Trust is basic but dangerous because there can be no trust without risk. For the hard truth is that trust, exactly because it is more fundamental than distrust, makes betrayal not only possible but likely. Even liars do not want to be lied to.

So we try to hedge our bets by trying to trust with reservation. Yet as creatures who desperately long to trust without reservation, we often abandon our self-protective strategies. If you do not believe that, ask yourself why, in spite of your often justified mistrust of others, you continue to want to be trusted. For it is surely the case that one mark of a trustworthy person is their desire to be trusted. That is why, in spite of our reservations, we trust people who trust themselves sufficiently to want to assume positions of responsibility. We do so because we sense there is an essential connection between authority and trust.

There are, of course, times and circumstances we think it impossible to trust ourselves or others. Some, indeed many, of us try to protect ourselves from the disappointment bred by betrayal by making cynicism a way of life. But cynics are caught in a terrible dilemma: Their cynicism reflects their desire to be a people of hope who, at the very least, can trust themselves. That is why you can never talk a cynic out of their cynicism by argument. Rather, what defeats the cynic is the realization that attempts to make cynicism a way of life cannot be lived.

Even if we fail to acknowledge how fundamentally trust sustains our lives, we find it difficult to imagine this or any world devoid of trust. Try, for example, to imagine a world whose landscape is shaped entirely by distrust. Even that part of the world we call politics is hard to imagine without trust. Of course it is true that tyrants (whose name may well be "the people") depend on their subjects not trusting one another. They do so because they understand that distrust is the breeding ground for the assumption that someone must rule if we are to survive a world without trust. But even tyrants want to be trusted.

Such a world of distrust is well on display in the book of Esther. The drama of Esther takes place against the background of the Persian Empire dominated by King Ahasuerus. Ahasuerus's decrees are the only law of the land. The problem is that Ahasuerus's rule is so arbitrary, he cannot even remember his own decrees. It is not clear if his "forgetfulness" is calculated or not, but what is clear is that his arbitrariness ensures that no one can be trusted, which means that all power begins and ends with Ahasuerus.

Power so conceived must be displayed in order to reinforce the presumption that there is no limit to what the one possessing the power wishes to do. Ahasuerus, therefore, spends enormous resources and time giving banquets that seem to have no purpose other than making clear that those who come to the banquet are beholden to the king. That his power comes from the breeding ground of distrust is why his close advisors must be eunuchs who cannot desire to be king. Yet, as is often the case, the king is at the mercy of such advisors, having made himself incompetent by knowing only what they tell him. Thus Ahasuerus is willing to let his high official, Haman, in an effort to eliminate all threats to Haman's power, plan to execute Mordecai and the Jews. Murder, it seems, is the natural outgrowth of the politics of distrust and betrayal.

The Jews' only hope is Esther. Esther is an orphan who has been adopted by her uncle Mordecai. Her adoption may be the only act of trust in the book of Esther. Beautiful and sexual, she has become Ahasuerus's queen. But even the queen cannot appear before Ahasuerus without being summoned. To do so risks death unless the king touches her with his golden scepter. Esther appears before Ahasuerus, is touched by his scepter, and begs him to spare her and her people. Ahasuerus grants her request; Haman is hung on the gallows meant for Mordecai and Mordecai is given Haman's position in the king's court.

So we are left with a happy ending that Mordecai decrees should be remembered every year by the Jews at a set time. Why? Because by remembering this story, the Jews are reminded of the time they triumphed over their enemies. Moreover, they are reminded of *how* they triumphed. Just as Mordecai trusted Esther to use her position of power to save her people, any Jew, regardless of political status, must embody Esther's courage and willingness to set aside her privilege for the sake of the other. Jews must trust one another, for such trust is quite literally necessary for survival.

By now you may well be wondering: What do these philosophical ramblings about trust as well as this strange story of how Esther saved the Jews have to do with Founder's Day? I think the point quite simply is this: This is the day we are asked to keep trust with the trust that has made us Duke University. To be asked to remember our benefactors can be interpreted by cynics as but our way of holding an Ahasuerus-like banquet. But I think that interpretation would be a deep mistake, betraying who we are as well as those we serve.

To keep trust with the trust that has made us is an obligation we dare not fail to meet, even if the university we have become is quite different than the one James B. Duke and President Few imagined. This university is an institution entrusted with the task of remembering the gifts that have made this world something other than the world of Ahasuerus. The university is, after all, the institution committed to giving the dead a voice.

In the indenture naming, as well as providing for, Duke University, Mr. Duke observed: "I recognize that education, when conducted along sane and practical, as opposed to dogmatic and theoretical lines, is, next to religion, the greatest civilizing influence." Whatever one may think about how Mr. Duke understood the distinction between practical and theoretical reason, I think he was not wrong to insist that the university that keeps trust with trust not only is a civilizing institution but exemplifies what it means to be civil.

For the university to be so entrusted does not mean that every expectation of our founders must be met. To keep trust with the trust that made us Duke University means we can be no less courageous and imaginative than those who entrusted us to represent and continue the work of this university. Indeed, one of the sure ways a trust is betrayed is by doing no more than meeting the letter of the law. It is our good fortune to have founders who saw that if the South was to free itself of slavery, a university must exist capable of providing a future otherwise unimaginable. In a war-weary world, we dare not be any less imaginative.

I should like to think that the university, and Duke University in particular, is an alternative to that ultimate form of mistrust we call war. The university is, so to speak, a safe haven where it is possible to make articulate the conflicts inherent in our lives in the hope that, through argument, we may learn to trust one another. This commitment I take to be as true for the sciences as it is for the humanities. Just ask yourself how betrayed you felt when a scientist "cooked" his results. The university, and the world in which we find ourselves, depends on us to be people who trust one another to say what we take to be true. For, as odd as it may seem, truth honed from conflict can be an alternative to war.

I have not forgotten this is a sermon. Yet you may have noticed I have not mentioned the name of God. I have good precedent for that oversight. Esther is one of the few books of the Bible in which the name of God does not appear. In Esther, God does not miraculously appear to save the Jews. God seems to have left it up to the Jews, and in particular to Mordecai and Esther, to accomplish that task. Jews without wit for survival are surely a people in desperate trouble. But Esther is a book of wit for survival.

God, it seems, trusts his people. He even trusts his people to risk trusting themselves. He trusts his people to have in the canon of scripture a book that tells a fascinating story with no indication that they have been made who they are by God's promise. Rather than spelling it out, it is the very witness of the Jews, and in particular of Esther and Mordecai, that makes clear God can be trusted to be God.

That God, the God who made heaven and earth, is praised by the Psalmist because God's trustworthiness has made it possible for Israel to escape "like a bird from the fowlers' snare" (Psalm 124:7). The Psalms were written and sung by a people who had to learn through the ages to live out of control. They learned to so live because they knew, often with knowledge painfully earned, that God can be trusted to be God. That trust made it possible for God's people, often under terrible threats, to continue to have children. With the birth of every child, the Jews witness their conviction that their very existence is not a mistake. They have, moreover, a tradition of trust to pass on to every generation.

But this is a Christian chapel and this is a Christian pulpit. I am a Christian. Surely Christians must have something to say about the role of the university. I believe we do have something to say, but it must be said very carefully. The university began as an expression of the Christian imagination. Christians had and continue to have a stake in universities even if we are no longer in control of universities like Duke that had a Christian foundation. But I think it was a mistake for Christians to think they could only trust universities they controlled.

Sam Wells identifies that time when Christians presumed control of the university as the prologue to a three-chapter story. The first chapter was the period early in the last century when the churches traded their theological identity to retain institutional influence. Chapter two is the period of significant social change in which there was a revolt against privilege and hierarchy that rendered Christian identity problematic, particularly in universities. We live in chapter three, which Wells characterizes as a battleground that as yet does not have an undisputed narrative of its own.

At least one aspect that characterizes chapter three, according to Wells, is the Christian lamentation over the loss of "their universities." Wells argues that for Christians to indulge in such a lament is a mistake not only because there is no "going back," but, more important, the presumption of control has robbed Christians of their ability to live by their wits. For Wells, if Christians can give up their desire to be in control, if Christians can learn to trust that God is here in the work of this university even when God's name is absent, we might discover again what it means to live as Christians whose very lives depend on our trust in a trustworthy Lord.

In our Gospel lesson for today, the disciples ask Jesus what they should do about people who are casting out demons in the name of Jesus but who do not seem to be card-carrying members of the Jesus movement. Jesus tells the disciples to leave them alone because what they do in his name is of service to the kingdom. That seems like good advice for Christians at this time in the ongoing life of the university. Let us resist the temptation to secure our control of the university by tactics of fear, coercion, or manipulation. Instead, let us learn to live by our wits. To so live takes courage and requires that we trust in God and one another. Who knows? If Christians learn to live and think as a people who trust God to be God, we may well discover we have something so interesting to say that our non-Christian university colleagues will be glad we exist because they can trust us to be a people of trust.

PART IV

Sermons on the Priesthood

15

A Priestly People

St. Luke's Episcopal Church Atlanta, Georgia
In Celebration of the Twentieth Anniversary
of Father Dan Matthews's Ordination
Delivered September 19, 2010

Numbers 11:16–17, 24–25
Psalm 27:4–6
Ephesians 4:7, 11–16
Matthew 9:35–38

God knows we need priests. I am a theologian but even I know we need priests because I am first and foremost a layperson. My highest ecclesial status is as the spouse of one ordained. My wife is an ordained United Methodist minister. Her bishop has appointed her to the Church of the Holy Family, an Episcopal Church, in Chapel Hill, North Carolina. Bishop Curry, the bishop of North Carolina, has approved of her ministry at Holy Family. If I am asked if I believe in the priesthood my only response is I do not have to believe in the priesthood because I have seen it enacted in my wife.

My sense of the importance of the priesthood for the church has been heightened because the Church of the Holy Family recently lost our rector, Timothy Kimbrough, who had served us for twenty-one years. He resigned to become dean of the Cathedral in Nashville, Tennessee. I am honored that the vestry asked me to serve on the search committee for the new rector of Holy Family. To be on a search committee in the Episcopal Church turns out to be a full-time job, but it is a job well worth the time and energy required.

Service on a search committee can make one aware of some very sobering realities. It does not take great familiarity with current ecclesial practices to learn how a less-than-capable priest can, in fairly short order, ruin a thriving congregation. I have developed a good deal of skepticism about the current psychoanalytic models concerning the codependency between rector and congregation, but it remains true that the character of a congregation often reflects the character of its priest. Of course, it also works the other way as priests learn how to be priests from those they serve. These are subtle matters we often prefer to leave unacknowledged.

But it is a good and right thing that you do not want to leave unacknowledged the joy Father Matthews's priesthood gives you. St. Luke's is obviously a thriving congregation well served by Father Matthews. Twenty years as a priest is no small thing. That you would want to celebrate the twentieth anniversary of his ordination is completely appropriate. Yet I feel sure that Father Matthews would want you first and foremost to celebrate that which makes his ordination intelligible, that is, that his priesthood, as Paul puts it in Ephesians, is not his but rather is a gift of Christ. What it means for the priesthood, indeed what it means for all the gifts Paul mentions, to be measured by Christ's gift is well worth pondering.

That we are directed by the church to read this passage from Ephesians on the occasion of the Ordination of a Priest is curious. Though Paul tells us that among the gifts that Christ will give the church are apostles, prophets, evangelists, pastors, and teachers, this division of labor is not Paul's primary concern. Rather, Paul is concerned that the church at Ephesus be united in the love that comes only by speaking the truth. Paul's designation of the various offices, offices determined by "the measure of Christ's gift," are meant to help us be a people capable of speaking the truth in love so that we might be united in service to one another and the world.

The church at Ephesus has clearly not been free of divisions. Crafty, deceitful, scheming people have used trickery to make these folk who are young in the faith think they must believe this or that doctrine. That some are set aside to be apostles, prophets, evangelists, pastors, and teachers is to help the church grow up. I do not believe by "being grown" Paul meant that there can be no disputes in the church, but rather that the disputes we have must not lead to our refusal to worship the same Lord. Thus, Paul insists that the diversity of gifts in the church at Ephesus should knit the body together in the bond of peace that comes from the recognition that Christ is the head of the church.

Indeed, while Paul is concerned about the unity of the church and the priestly roles some are called to take on to sustain that unity, his concern springs from the affirmation that we have only one true priest, Jesus Christ. That Christ is now our one true priest means we are at once similar yet different from those God called to be his promised people, that is, Israel. Like Israel before us, we are called to be a priestly people. Out of all the people of the world, God made Israel his possession not because all people do not belong to Israel's God, but because God chose Israel to be God's representative to all people, just as Israel was to represent our humanity before God.

Through law and sacrifice, Israel was called to be a holy people. Accordingly, some were set aside to be priests to offer daily sacrifices. The sacrifices had to be offered daily because Israel knew that the sacrifices she offered, sacrifices made to God in the hope that God's sin-disrupted order could be restored, were never adequate. But we believe that in the crucifixion of Jesus, a sacrifice has been made that has ended all other sacrifices. Jesus has exercised a priesthood that only he could exercise by his willingness to be the priest who is sacrificed on our behalf.

No person will ever again be a priest in the sense that Jesus is our one true priest. In Christ we now have one High Priest who has once and for all offered the perfect and adequate sacrifice. Yet by his priestly action, we are united with him, becoming thereby his priestly people. The church occupies the space he has made so that the world may see what a people look like who are not determined by the destructive fantasy that we can secure our lives through violence.

But if the one priesthood in the church is that of Christ himself, why then are some ordained to be priests? Does not setting aside some to be priests risk creating divisions in the church that betray the unity of our common task? Paul says the answer to this question is "no." Rather, some are set aside to be priests because we need someone to do for us what only the whole church can do. Priests are ordained not for their salvation but rather to enact the salvation that is ours through baptism into the death and resurrection of Christ. So to ordain a priest is to establish an order in the community in which the whole community is the recipient of the gift that is Christ.

Priests are to baptize, preside at the Eucharist, read and interpret scripture, and lead a life of prayer. Priests are also privileged to be with us in our most vulnerable moments; they are present as we die, at the celebration of marriage and birth, when we feel betrayed by those we had come to trust. No doubt by being so exposed, they may become better human beings, but they are present to us at such times because they bring the whole church with them. That is why we as a church can trust even the young and inexperienced priest to be with us in times of sadness and joy.

Do not miss, therefore, that what we do today, that is, celebrate a priest's twenty years of ministry in the church of Jesus Christ, is a radical political act. Such a claim may seem quite odd. Twenty years of faithful service is certainly quite significant, but not all that unusual. Some people even stay married for twenty years. What could possibly be so radical about such a celebration?

But what we do here today is radical insofar as it makes clear that we are not individuals who happen to show up once a week to convince ourselves that the eccentric opinions we hold are not that odd. Rather we are a people, as Rowan Williams suggests, whose imagination is constantly renewed by a celebratory sharing in the great narratives that hold them together, the narratives of God's actions which have brought them close to each other and whose resonances they recognize in each other.[1]

The world in which we find ourselves is dying to have what we have been given. The world longs to have a politics in which those called to serve their communities do not have to be "strong leaders." For the problem with "strong leaders" is they cannot help but base their authority on the deficiency of the community they serve. They must make those they serve less so that they can be more. They must be "heroic."

But those called to the priesthood are not called to be heroic. They are not even called to be strong. Rather they are

---

1. Rowan Williams, *Tokens of Trust: An Introduction to Christian Belief* (Louisville, KY: Westminster John Knox Press, 2010), 112–13.

called to be faithful. They are called to be holy. They are called to celebrate the common acts that make it possible for us to be a people across time and space to be in unity with one another. They are called to remind us that we have all the time in the world to be patient with those with whom we disagree so that we may discover the goods that come through our common worship of a crucified savior.

I am aware that all this may sound abstract, if not idealistic. However let me make it as concrete as I can by calling attention to our former archbishop, Rowan Williams. Rowan Williams's hesitancy to impose a unity on the church has frustrated many. For example, in his otherwise quite favorable biography of Rowan Williams, *Rowan's Rule*, Rupert Shortt criticizes the archbishop for being politically naïve, particularly when it comes to the necessary exercise of power. As a result of that naïveté, Shortt suggests, the archbishop is often outmaneuvered by his opponents in the messy world of church politics. Yet such an account of "Rowan's rule" I think fails to do justice to Rowan Williams's understanding of what it means to receive the gift of the priesthood from Christ.

For the measure of Christ's gift we have been given is the cross. The cross was necessary because God refuses to force or coerce us to love him. The cross is that focal moment in which the divine relinquishes claims against humanity and the human accepts the full consequences of the divine presence in a violent world. That is the truth we must speak to one another in love. That is the defenseless form of authority Rowan Williams has exercised as our archbishop. Rowan Williams loves God and, God help him, he loves the church he leads. Therefore he refuses to force us to "get along." Instead he keeps us focused on the essential acts of the church in the hope that we might be "joined and knit together" so that the world might see what it means for a people to love one another.

That Rowan Williams has refused the role of a strong leader I believe, moreover, is of service not only to the church but to the world. A priest, after all, is not a prisoner of the church, but is, like all Christians, called to be of service to the world. But, again as Rowan Williams reminds us, we are not a people of faith because we want to make a contribution to civic life, we are a people of faith because we believe what we believe is true. What could be of greater service to the world, then, than to be a people who want to have our priests tell us the truth—even when the truth means admitting that they do not have the answers we seek? Rather than simply providing answers to life's puzzling questions, the gift of the priest to the community is what they do: They baptize, preside at the Eucharist, and preach, in the full confidence that by doing so God will make us his priestly people.

I am sure that at least one of the reasons you celebrate Dan Matthews's ordination anniversary is that he also has kept you focused on the essential acts of the church. For without those acts, we will not know how to speak the truth to one another in love. Without those acts, we would not even know what the truth is. Without those acts, we would be subject to the manipulative politics that believes there is no truth. To celebrate, therefore, twenty years of service as a priest is no small thing.

God knows we need priests. God knows we need priests like Rowan Williams and Dan Matthews. God knows that without them we are lost. But they exist. They exist because you, a priestly people, exist. Praise God. We are not without hope.

16

Clothe Your Ministers with Righteousness

Duke Divinity School
Ordination of Nathaniel Lee
Delivered February 2, 2011

Isaiah 6:1–8
Psalm 132:8–18
1 Peter 5:1–4
John 10:11–18

Soon, Nathaniel Lee, you will be made a priest. It is my duty to tell you what God is going to do to you. I do so though I am a layman. But it may be that we, the laity, are well positioned to tell you what it means for you to be made a priest. We are well positioned because we know how much our lives depend on your being a priest. It is not without reason at Morning Prayer we pray: "Clothe your ministers with righteousness; Let your people sing with joy." If our ministers get it wrong, we are unable to sing. If our priests are not clothed with righteousness, it seems our very salvation is in doubt.

I have, moreover, spent the last year serving on the rector search committee for the Church of the Holy Family. To serve on a rector search committee is a full-time job. It is a full-time job because we on the committee think that the task we have been given is crucial if Holy Family is to be a church that is pleasing to God. We prayed, therefore, not that God would send us someone we liked, but that God would help us discern the one God had chosen to lead us.

I confess that I found my participation on the committee inspiring and humbling. I was inspired by the faith of my colleagues on the committee. I was inspired by the process, which was primarily determined by prayer. I am a layperson but because I am a theologian, I get paid to believe. My colleagues on the committee believe what they believe because it obviously makes such a difference for their lives. I am humbled, if not humiliated, by such lives.

I also discovered that the Episcopal Church is a congregational polity with bishops. You will soon be asked if you will respect and be guided by the pastoral direction and leadership of your bishop. That is surely right and good, ensuring, as it does, our catholicity. But I think you will also discover that you are surrounded by laypeople who will make Christ present to you in a manner you often have not anticipated. I suspect at times you will find this frightening just to the extent you will feel out of control.

But to be a priest is to occupy an office that requires the one holding the office to learn to live perpetually out of control. After tonight, your life will be constituted by the invocation of the Holy Spirit to make this bread and this wine the body and blood of Christ. At the very least, that means you will never be in control of your life invocating, as you must, a God so wild to make of you and us participants in the alternative reality called the Kingdom of God.

So let me put it to you, Nathaniel Lee, as straight as I can. You are going to be made a priest. The language we rightly use is "consecration." To consecrate is to dedicate you to God. This is going to change your life. Put even more dramatically: From this moment till you die all that you are and all that you do will be determined by your being a priest. To be a priest does not mean you have a job that ends at the end of the day. Rather, to be a priest means that you will go to bed as a priest, you will wake up as a priest, you will buy groceries as a priest, you will make jokes as a priest, you will study as a priest. From this time on, there is no time when you are not a priest.

I suspect we often think that few events in our lives are more life-changing than when we marry or have children. Those events are surely significant, but to be made a priest entails even a more determinative change in one's life than marriage or having children. To be married or to have children certainly feels all-consuming, but we can rightly have aspects of our lives that are not determined by our being married or by our having children. That is not the case once you are made a priest.

That is why some in the Christian tradition have suggested the change in the life of a person ordained to the priesthood is properly described as "ontological." You may wonder if what is to happen to you has such metaphysical significance, but I would encourage you not to dismiss the possibility of that reality. At the very least, to use a word as strange as "ontological" to describe the change your consecration as a priest entails is a good reminder that what is done to you "goes all the way down."

That you are first and foremost a priest I hope, moreover, will save you from the unhappy presumption, a presumption widespread in our day, that you must choose between a ministry that is prophetic or one that is primarily pastoral. That unhappy choice seems written into the contemporary DNA of the ministry. Those who assume the mantle of the prophet are thought incapable of being pastoral. The reverse is also assumed to be true. Thus the presumption that those who make time to be with the sick, to care for the dying, to exercise non-threatening leadership cannot be prophetic. You have to be one or the other.

This division is legitimated by seminary curriculums just to the extent the work done in scripture, historical theology, church history, and theology is said to be academic, but the work done in the ministerial division is described as "pastoral." Such an alternative, an alternative that becomes an antagonism, serves no one well. I am a pacifist, but you have my permission to make life difficult for anyone who tells you, "They do not care what you know. They want to know you care." Never forget the care you provide turns out to depend on what you know because the care you provide must be shaped by the cross and resurrection of Christ.

The scriptures appointed for today can be read in a manner that underwrites the separation of the prophetic from the pastoral. I have sometimes suspected that the use of Isaiah 6 at ordinations is the equivalent of 1 Corinthians 13 being read at weddings. I think that to use Isaiah 6 at ordinations may be at least as misleading as the use of 1 Corinthians 13 at weddings. First Corinthians 13 is not first about marriage, but about the love Christ has made possible between Christians—thus my observation that Christians, even if they are married, must love one another not because they are married but because they are Christians. The corresponding misunderstanding of Isaiah 6 is that those called to be prophets do not have to be priests.

I do not want to be misunderstood. I am quite sympathetic with those who are to be ordained identifying with Isaiah. No doubt few feel worthy of being made a priest. No doubt most think it is only through the grace of God that they can say, "Here am I; send me." But God called Isaiah to be a prophet. His call was not, as most prophetic calls are not, a happy one. Isaiah was to say to the people, "Keep listening, but do not comprehend; keep looking, but do not understand." Isaiah was called to be a prophet. He was not called to be a priest.

Yet our Christ is the end of prophecy. Because Christ is the fulfillment of Israel's hopes, you do not have to choose between being a prophet and being a priest. Such a choice betrays the reality that the church is a prophetic community necessary for the world to know that God refuses to abandon us. We are God's hope for the world. You are a servant of that hope. That you are so will be indelibly stamped on your soul every time you are given the gift to be present with us as we die.

Your task, as we are told in 1 Peter, is "to tend the flock of God that is in your charge, exercising the oversight, not under compulsion but willingly, as God would have you do it—not for sordid gain but eagerly." Then comes the hard part: "Do not lord it over those in your charge." That is clearly not good advice for the ambitious who want to get something done. But Peter assumes that Christ has done all that needs to be done. What now must be done is for us to be a people capable of recognizing in you our Christ and you recognizing in those you serve the same Christ. That is how and why the prophetic and pastoral tasks become one in your priesthood.

You will soon be asked if you will "undertake to be a faithful pastor to all whom you are called to serve, laboring together with them and with your fellow ministers to build up the family of God." That sounds "pastoral." That sounds "caring." But I assure you that is what it means to be prophetic. That is what it means to be called to be a shepherd for a people who would not have leaders who lord it over them. That is what it means to be a priest.

For what we most need from you, as you are made a priest, is to be with us. What we need most from you is constant faithfulness. We know we are a church in a mess. Do not abandon us. We know we are often unfaithful. Do not abandon us. We know our lives are dominated by our fear of death. Do not abandon us.

The hired hand runs away when the wolf snatches one of us from the flock. He runs away because he does not care for us. But you must love us. For you must be for us what we are called to be for the world, that is, a people formed into the image of Christ. In your priesthood we must see ourselves reflected and you must see who you are by looking on us.

This is as serious as it gets. After today there is no time, no place, no relationship, no task when you will not be a priest. You must and will represent Christ for us so that we may be Christ's representatives for the world. This is not an everyday affair. This is not regular. This is the work of the Holy Spirit invading this life, the life of Nathaniel Lee, to make his life our life. Praise God for the gift of this life for without such gifts we perish.

17

Because It Is True

Seminary of the Southwest
Commencement
Delivered May 8, 2012

Exodus 19:3–8
Psalm 15
Matthew 16:24–27

Because it is true. On this celebratory occasion, an occasion that is at once an end and a beginning, my prayer for you is that in the future, when you are asked why you came to seminary, why you sought ordination, why you were willing to be a priest in a confused and compromised church, or even why you are a Christian, all you will be able to say is, "Because it is true." That all you can say is, "Because it is true," may mean you have had a difficult life, that is, a life stripped of what many associate with standards of success. Yet I side with the Psalmist, who insists that those who would abide in the Lord's tent must "speak the truth from their heart." "Because it is true" is the necessary condition for such speech.

I do not mean to suggest that if your life has been successful, or at least happy, you have failed to speak heartfelt truth. But we live in a time when Christians are tempted to make truth irrelevant for why anyone might consider being a Christian. Faced with the church's declining membership and status, a cottage industry has developed to entice people to give Christianity a try. These strategies for church growth are designed to work in a manner that makes irrelevant questions of truth. I have no reason to deny that being a Christian may give your life meaning—whatever that may mean or whatever good it may do—may save your marriage, or even get you to work on time, but it is also the case that to speak the truth from the heart may disrupt our presumptions of success.

Of course it is not only Christians who have given up on truth. Voltaire no longer thought he needed God as an explanatory hypothesis. In the same spirit, Richard Rorty, one of our most distinguished contemporary philosophers, argued that truth is not a concept needed to sustain the work of philosophy or science. Nietzsche gave this denial of truth classical expression when he observed:

> What then is truth? A movable host of metaphors, metonymies, and anthropomorphisms: in short, a sum of human relations which have been poetically and rhetorically intensified, transferred and embellished, and which, after long usage, seem to people to be fixed, canonical and binding. Truths are illusions we have forgotten are illusions; they are metaphors that have become worn out and have been drained of sensuous force, coins which have lost their embossing and are now considered as metal and no longer as coins.[1]

This eloquent denial of truth earned Nietzsche the characterization "nihilist." But, ironically, he was anything but a nihilist. At least, he was not a nihilist if you acknowledge that he was, in fact,

---

1. Quoted in Alasdair MacIntyre, *The Rival Versions of Moral Enquiry: Encyclopedia, Genealogy, and Tradition* (Notre Dame: University of Notre Dame Press, 1990), 35.

passionately committed to living a life free of self-deception. As he wrote in *The Gay Science,* the "'will to truth' does not mean 'I do not want to let myself be deceived' but—there is no alternative—'I will not deceive, not even myself'; and with that we stand on moral ground."[2] Yet, Nietzsche knew that living free of deception must be an ongoing struggle, for we so love the lie. Nietzsche is a witness Christians dare not ignore.

Nietzsche was surely right to observe that we do not like to be deceived, but it is also true that we wish others to regard us more highly than we deserve. That is why Pascal observes that we hate the truth and those who would tell us the truth. We desire that others be deceived in our favor; that is, we want to be esteemed by others in a manner that confirms the illusions we harbor to sustain our life projects. That is why, Pascal suggests, few friendships would endure if each friend knew what was said by their friends in their absence. According to Pascal, it is a fact that if everyone knew what was said of them by others, there would not be four friends in the world.

From Pascal's perspective, human society is founded on mutual deceit because our loves, and in particular our self-love, requires that we hide the truth from one another and from ourselves. We fear wounding one another with the truth because we so desperately want to be loved. We do not wish, therefore, for anyone to tell us the truth and we avoid telling it to others. These habits of deception become rooted in the heart, making it impossible for us to speak truthfully.

I fear you will find Pascal's account of deceit all too relevant for your calling as a priest. After all, you are a human being. You

---

2. Friedrich Neitzsche, *The Gay Science: With a Prelude in Rhymes and an Appendix of Songs,* trans. Walter Kaufmann (New York: Random House, 1974), 282.

will want to be loved by those you serve. In particular, you will be called to be present to your people when their lives are in crisis. Do not be surprised, however, because you have been present at such times: Those to whom you have been present will find it difficult to love you. Because you are a priest, you will be welcomed by people even when they are without protection and have no way to disguise their vulnerability. In the midst of the crisis you will be loved, or at least admired, for your presence and care. But after the crisis is over, you will discover that the very intimacy established between you and those to whom you were present now means they fear what you know of them. You have been allowed to see truthfully who they are, which will often mean that they want as much distance from you as they can get.

To sustain a community capable of having the lies that constitute our lives exposed, to sustain the practice of speaking the truth from the heart requires, as our Psalmist suggests, the creation of a people who do not slander one another. Rather, they are people with a genius for friendship, refusing to do evil to their friends. Nor do they reproach their neighbors, because they honor all who fear the Lord. They stand by their oath even when it is not to their advantage, and they do not lend money at interest or take bribes against the innocent. The Psalmist seems to suggest these are the necessary conditions for a community of trust because without trust we are incapable of being truthful to ourselves. And if we are incapable of being truthful to ourselves, we will eventually discover that we cannot be truthful to one another.

For Christians, the truth that makes such trust possible is no abstract truth. The truth that makes possible truthful speech, heartfelt speech, is a person. The "it" in "because it is true" is a person. Truth for us is not a principle or system, not a structure of correct insights, not a doctrine. The expression of the truth may use any of these means to say what is true, but as Barth rightly insists, "Jesus Christ in the promise of the Spirit as His revelation in the sphere of our time and history is the truth."[3] Only in the person of Christ are we encountered by the One who can unmask our illusions without utterly destroying us. In Christ we are made intimate with God, making possible a nearness from which we do not flee.

Jesus is the truth that judges and tests all other truths that would seek to be established independent of the love shown to us in Christ. Accordingly, any attempt to judge Jesus by a theory of truth not determined by cross and resurrection can only tempt us to think we are the measure of what is true. Jesus is, as Barth maintains, the true witness who does not need to be confirmed or authorized by any other truth. Rather he is the truth from which all other claims of truth are to be judged. "He is the true Witness. He is Himself the truth and its expression. And in His existence and life as such He unmasks every other man."[4]

Jesus is the heart from which the truth must be spoken. Thus, the truth that must be spoken is known only through witness. Because he is the truth, we can speak the truth. That speaking the truth takes the form of witness means we are confronted with this truth in a manner that does not allow us to distance ourselves from him. Any attempt to sunder truth from this, the true witness, to make truth an idea about the relation between God and man, cannot be the truth. If the truth is thought to be but a symbol, no matter how exalted, it is but a falsehood. The true witness is this man of Gethsemane and Golgotha.

---

3. Karl Barth, *Dogmatics in Outline* (New York: Harper Torchbooks, 1959), 130.

4. Ibid.

Because the truth is this person, the One who endured Gethsemane and Golgotha, it is a truth that cannot resort to coercion to secure its status. The truth that is Christ, the truth that can only be known by witness, is a truth that must make its way in the world by refusing to use the desperate means of the world to force others to acknowledge what is claimed to be true. There can be nothing desperate about the witness that is Christ because what God has done through the Son cannot be undone. That is why the truth that is Christ is so compelling. It is compelling because those possessed by this truth are filled with joy.

But then, what are we to make of our Gospel for today, in which we are told that any who would be a follower of Jesus must take up their cross and follow him? What are we to make of Jesus' claim that those who would save their lives must be willing to lose their lives? I confess I cannot think of any advice more destructive for those called to the priesthood. Such advice cannot help but tempt you to think that your calling is sufficient for you to believe you are making a sacrifice of the self. Such a presumption, unfortunately, is a formula for priests to try to secure their status and power by becoming proficient at playing the game of passive-aggressive behavior.

Jesus, however, does not say that to live sacrificially is a good in and of itself. Rather he says that those who lose their life *for my sake* will find their life. "For my sake" means that we are invited to be a witness to the witness that is Jesus. That witness, to be sure, may require a sacrifice, but if the sacrifice is to be true, it must not point to itself but to Jesus. It is the cross of Christ that is the sacrifice that has ended all sacrifices other than those whose end is Christ. By the grace of God we are invited to share in Christ's sacrifice, but such a sharing makes possible lives no longer captured by our self-deceptive strategies to secure our own significance. The appropriate description for lives so determined is joy.

Joy is the mark of lives shaped by the truth that is Christ. To be captivated by such a truth—to be, as the Psalmist suggests, a heartfelt speaker of the truth—means those so determined will "never be moved." To "never be moved" is the Psalmist's way of saying that those whose lives are determined by Christ can be trusted to be who they say they are. "Sincerity" and "integrity" are not sufficient to describe such people. Steadfast, I think, is closer to the mark. They are who they are by the grace of God.

What a wonderful time to be a Christian. What a wonderful time to serve the Christian people. Odd sentiments if, as I suggested above, the church seems to be in a downward spiral. Yet, that this is the case simply means we have nothing to lose by speaking the truth to ourselves, one another, and the world. It is surely the case that the world is dying—quite literally—for a people capable of speaking the truth from their heart. It is true that truth in our time is obscure and falsehood is well established, but that is no reason for us to despair of truthful speech. After all, God, through his Son, has shown us that to desire the truth requires loving the truth. For without love we cannot know the truth that moves the sun and the stars.

So I end where I began, that is, I pray that when you are asked why you came to seminary, or later when you reflect on why you have given your life in service to the church, that is to say, why you have lived your life as a Christian, the only reason you have left to give—and it is a sufficient reason—is, "Because it is true."

18

Good Work

Nashotah House
Commencement
Delivered May 24, 2012

Exodus 15:22–25
Psalm 67
1 Corinthians 3:8–11
Matthew 28:16–20

We were at the end of a long day of intense conversation. At the behest of Alonzo McDonald, who had been kind enough to help fund a sabbatical for me, a group of my friends were gathered to tell me what I should do before I die or, at least, on my sabbatical. Toward the end of the day, one friend, who is not a Christian, expressed his admiration for the Christianity my friends represented even though he did not understand what it meant for them to be so identified. I found myself saying in response: "I am happy to be a Christian because being a Christian gives me something to do."

I was not then nor am I now sure what led me to blurt out "it gives me something to do," but the more I have thought about what I said, the more I think what I said to be right and true. By "right and true," I mean that to say being a Christian gives us something to do is not only true for me, but for anyone who would be a Christian. We are not just happy to be Christians, but we have discovered that being a Christian makes us happy because we have something to do.

Happy, of course, is far too weak a word in our culture to describe what it means to be a Christian. "Having something to do" is far more important than being happy. It is so because for Christians to have something to do means we have good work to do. To have good work means we have been—and continue to be—given tasks to perform, tasks that often are not of our own choosing, for the common life of the people of God. The heart of the work we are given to do, or perhaps better put, the animating center of all we do as Christians, is the worship of God.

You may think it quite odd to call worship a form of work. Worship is often compared to play; that is, it is assumed that worship is effortless activity with no other purpose than praise of God. In contrast, work is what you do when you need to get something done. I was raised a bricklayer. Laying brick is work. Indeed, laying brick is very hard and demanding physical work. You lay brick because this building needs to be built. Accordingly, if laying brick is work, then to call worship work seems to be a category mistake.

I suspect the contrast between laying brick and worship is one of the reasons I have wondered if as an academic, and in particular, an academic who is a theologian, I have ever had to work for a living. I have been, and continue to be, paid for reading books and thinking about God. That does not sound like work. I get paid, admittedly not much, for writing books. Writing, which is but a form of thinking, can be quite difficult but I suspect many people would not think writing to be work. I am also a teacher, but again it is not clear that teaching, though teaching can be quite physically tiring, is properly thought of as work.

The difference between theology as work and work that entails physical labor is indicated by how you feel when you have come to a stopping place. Whatever it may mean for theology to be work, you never have the satisfaction in the work of theology that comes from laying brick. At the end of a day spent laying brick, you get off the scaffold, look at the wall that now exists where there was nothing before you began the day, and you think, "I did that and it is not too bad." When you are a theologian and/or a teacher of theology there is never "a wall" that gives you that kind of satisfaction. You may have written this essay or given that lecture, but because you never seem to say what you thought you needed to say theologically in this essay or that lecture you can never be sure you have finished anything—including this sermon.

I make these observations about my life and whether what I do can be called "work" because I think you may well find that the same frustrations characterize what you are called to do as a priest. Many of the people you serve will assume that you do not have to work for a living. You are paid not to work in order that you will be available if they need you. As a result, your life may feel as if you are being nibbled to death by ducks. Many of the people you serve will assume you work, at best, one day a week. And even given that assumption, neither you nor they are sure that what you do on that day is properly understood as work.

One of the deepest frustrations entailed by the work you do or will do as a priest is that so much that you do can never be seen. Again, there's no wall to point to as proof of your hours of labor. Few will know of the countless hours you have spent helping a family deal with alcoholism. The peace treaty you have somehow accomplished between the senior and junior wardens will not be acknowledged because for the treaty to work, the presumption must be maintained that there was no war between the senior and junior wardens.

Even if it is assumed that as a priest you have work to do, it is by no means clear what that work may be. As H. Richard Niebuhr observed in 1956 in his book *The Purpose of the Church and Its Ministry*,[1] to be ordained to preach and preside at the Eucharist no longer seems to name the work that constitutes what is central for the ministry. Niebuhr even suggested a better name for ministers in our time would be "pastoral directors," because in effect, acknowledged or unacknowledged, the minister or priest works as an administrator, making it hard to distinguish what they do from the business manager who runs a non-profit enterprise. As a result, much of the training you receive in seminary, all the work you have done to be a good exegete, may seem to have prepared you for a job that does not exist.

So what can I possibly mean by suggesting that to be a Christian, and in particular a priest, means that we have been given good work to do? In his letter to the Corinthians, Paul clearly presumes that we are called to be laborers who participate in the common work given by God. To be a Christian, as Paul suggests to the Corinthians, is to be part of a people, each of whom has tasks that serve a common purpose. The one who plants and the one who waters are both necessary for God's garden, a garden in which we are at once the soil and those who work the soil so that food may be grown.

Paul even describes himself as a "skilled master builder." He is a worker who has laid a foundation for the church. That foundation is Jesus Christ. To have such a foundation makes the work we are called to do joyous. That Jesus Christ is the foundation of the

---

1. H. Richard Niebuhr, *The Purpose of the Church and Its Ministry,* (New York: Harper & Row, 1956).

church means that those who come after Paul do not have to start from scratch. Indeed, Paul notes that others are now building on the foundation he prepared. That is not a complaint, but rather Paul's sense of joy that a foundation has been laid that makes possible the building up of the church across time and space.

Paul observes that each builder will have to choose with care how to build on the foundation he has laid. Though a good foundation has been put in place, how to build on that foundation is not a given. Rather it seems that those who would follow Paul must develop the skills Paul must have had to be a master builder. This is good news because it means that we, like Paul, are not only given good work to do but we can be assured that it is good work because the foundation is true.

As a bricklayer, I can assure you that a foundation that is not true will play havoc with every aspect of the building. If the foundation is even a little off, the higher you go with your brick work, the more out of kilter everything becomes. The foundation may be off an inch, but by the time you get to sill level, that is, the space under the windows, you will discover you are now two inches off. The only way to make up the difference is to spread a bed joint that is a half-inch on one end and two inches on the other. And I can tell you from bitter experience that the result looks very bad, indeed.

You may worry that you are entering the priesthood in a church whose foundation is not true. There's no doubt we have problems, but they are problems identifiable because we have a sure foundation. You have been given good work to do because through your formation at Nashotah House you have discovered that you do not have to make Christianity up. All the work you have done to be a faithful reader of scripture has not been in vain.

You have done the work necessary to discover that the foundation has been laid. Your task, a happy task, is to choose with care how to build on what the master builders of the past have passed on to you. The good news is that you have been given something to do. You have work to do that has a purpose, in a world increasingly doubtful that the work we do can have any purpose other than a means to secure power over others.

It is quite interesting, and I think seldom noticed, that when the disciples saw Jesus on the mountain in Galilee some worshiped him, but some doubted. I think they did not doubt that Jesus was resurrected. I suspect they doubted whether they could comprehend in their living what it meant to worship Jesus. Jesus, however, refused their doubt by giving them good work to do. That work, the work of going to the nations baptizing them in the name of the Father and of the Son and of the Holy Spirit, is our work. It is work made possible because Jesus has the authority, an authority in which we share as his people, to commission us to be witnesses to the nations that they may know God's salvation.

I believe you are the most fortunate of human beings because there is no better work than the work of leading the people of God. The great good news is that your work is not pointless. The good news is that your work is not just busy work to keep you out of trouble. The good news is that the work you have been given is not yours alone. The good news is that the work you do will be built upon by others who care about the same things you care about. The good news is that the work we have been given does not depend only on ourselves, but we have been promised that God will call others to come after us to build on what we have done.

It is true that you will often find it hard to see any result from the work you have done. Even worse, you will sometimes see what you have worked hard to accomplish dismantled by those who come after you. But this is God's work. It is work that is impossible to sustain if we do not trust in God's determination to love us. God's building is built of small acts of kindness and tenderness that are themselves all the results we should desire. For as Sam Wells suggests in *God's Companions*,[2] God is a God of abundance who has given us all we need. We are not in a zero-sum game. Your life will not be wasted, because you have been made part of God's abundance.

You will be a priest for a lifetime. A lifetime is a long time. Your lives will be filled with disappointments, betrayals, meaningless struggles, and small and significant triumphs. The disappointments, betrayals, and the meaningless struggles are small things that will not threaten your lives if you remember you have been given something to do. You have been given good work that finds its central expression on Sunday morning when you are asked to represent God to the gathered community and to present the community to God. That is the work that makes all we do intelligible. I cannot imagine a life better lived.

---

2. Sam Wells, *God's Companions: Reimagining Christian Ethics* (Malden, MA: Blackwell, 2006).

PART V

Other Writings

19

Leadership

I confess I am not quite sure what to make of the recent avalanche of essays and books on leadership. In general I tend to be quite skeptical of "how-to" books, though I have no doubt that those who write books on how to do this or that may contain some wisdom. I have cherished a book found in a used bookstore written by someone named Donald Brann and titled *Bricklaying Simplified*. Mr. Brann does a nice job laying out the basics, but I cannot imagine how one could learn to lay brick by reading his book. You can only learn to lay brick by being initiated into the craft by a master craftsman.

Laying brick and assuming a position of leadership may seem like apples and oranges, but just as learning to lay brick requires that one become an apprentice, so does learning to assume a position of leadership. To lay brick and to be made responsible for the goods of a community require the development of practical wisdom because both laying brick and leadership involve judgments about matters that could be otherwise. For example, most of the time when laying brick you can do what you have always done, but one day you will discover you must do what you usually do differently because this corner, for example, has a unique angle. I suspect leadership entails similar challenges.

My sense that leadership requires the development of practical wisdom is one of the reasons I worry about the attempt to develop general theories about what makes a good or effective leader. Some generalizations may be possible, but given the diversity of societal and community contexts, what it means to "lead" cannot help but resist attempts to characterize leadership in general. Put differently, I worry that the focus on leadership qua leadership may undercut more basic descriptions of offices determined by a community's traditions, such as priest, president, teacher, parent, and physician. These descriptions should make a difference for the kind of judgments made, as well as the mode of discernment required to make the judgments, by those who are called to exercise "leadership" in a particular context and for particular ends.

I suspect the desire to develop general accounts of leadership is an expression of our loss of a positive account of authority. In the absence of any agreements about why we need offices of authority, leadership becomes a general category used to legitimize the power some have over others. Subsequently, leadership qua leadership implies some people rise to positions of power in order to "get things done" and not because such positions are inherently necessary to the common good. As a result, leadership reproduces the presumption that there is no alternative to the manipulative character of our interactions in modernity. The modern aversion to authority means modern people have to become convinced leadership is a good thing.

In his book *After Virtue*,[1] philosopher Alasdair MacIntyre argues that we find it difficult to know what non-manipulative interactions might look like because of the general presumption that all evaluations are arbitrary, as they can only express each person's peculiar sentiments. Because we believe our moral

---

1. Alasdair MacIntyre, *After Virtue* (Notre Dame: University of Notre Dame Press, 1981).

commitments to be no more than an expression of our "prefer-ences," any effort to have others join us in what we think needs to be done means we have no choice but to resort to manipula-tive bargaining strategies in the hope some will identify with our arbitrary choices.

MacIntyre invites us to recognize the implications of such a world by calling attention to three kinds of "social characters," which he argues reflect the moral and metaphysical presump-tions of our culture: the aesthete, the therapist, and the manager. The aesthete seeks to control others for their own entertain-ment; the therapist helps clients to become or do whatever they want to be or do without questioning their purposes; the manager uses the established bureaucracies to achieve its ends without ever calling into question those ends. I worry that the current focus on leadership may be a widespread cultural affir-mation of the social characters identified by MacIntyre.

MacIntyre's account of our social and political life may seem exaggerated, but confirmation of his account of our social and political lives can be readily found in the most recent commercial for this or that candidate running for public office. They always promise to provide "leadership." They promise, for example, to give us economic prosperity. What is missing is any acknowledg-ment that it is by no means clear that the office of the presidency of the United States has the power to make the economy do any-thing. Yet anyone running for office cannot acknowledge they are not quite sure what they would be able, as president, to do about the economy because such an acknowledgment would suggest that they are shirking the presumed responsibilities of being a "leader."

We are told, moreover, that the president is the "leader of the free world." What in the world does it mean for someone to be the leader of the free world? What or who do they lead as the leader of the free world? This attribution seems to imply that America embodies the ideal of freedom and that leadership is a matter of securing said freedom. But rather than promising us security, they might remind us that we live in a dangerous world that is quite beyond the control of anyone—even the president. The only alternative to the politics of manipulation is truth. But any leader who tells the truth stands little chance of being elected. As a nation, we demand truth while not having the courage to hear it.

What might all this have to do with the church? Am I implying that reflection about leadership in the church, i.e., how the church understands the politics that constitutes her life, is misguided? I certainly do not think that to be the case, but I do think the politics of the Gospel requires us to develop an account of leadership that stands as a challenge to the world in which we find ourselves. The church is to be a community that expects truth-telling from those who lead us, even if it means that the truth they must tell us is that they are not sure what the truth is in a given situation. And our leaders, moreover, are called to help us become the kind of people who can listen to truth because only the truth of Jesus Christ can truly set us free.

A community that demands of its leaders that they tell the truth is a community in which leadership is not a way to make up for the deficiencies of the community. Rather, leadership is necessary because the church is an institution constituted by the conviction that without truthful speech we cannot sustain the trust necessary to be a people who abide in Christ and one another. Accordingly, some are set aside to exercise the authority necessary to sustain the disciplines that make our abiding possible.

To exercise such authority is an exercise in power. Any community that cares about goods in common depends on offices of power, so it would be false to understand power and authority negatively. In the Gospels, Jesus is referred to as the Good Shepherd who cares for and tends to his flock. This is an image of power that entails a form of servanthood, i.e., caring and tending, and it is the image most aptly associated with leadership in the church. But this seemingly simple image is one Christians in positions of authority must struggle to understand if they are to represent it in their ministry. Failure to struggle with this Christological vision of leadership results in one of two dangerous positions. If the leader embraces a worldly form of power, their ministry will likely be just that, i.e., *their* ministry, rather than Christ's. This result takes the form of the parish becoming a cult of personality wherein parishioners rely on their leader's successes rather Christ. A sense of pride attaches to belonging to *this* pastor rather than *that* pastor, and the one Shepherd who leads the one flock becomes largely irrelevant. On the other hand, if a position of servanthood is assumed that precludes an acknowledgment of power, the same result happens, only with typically different outcomes. The servant who leads without acknowledging her power is too often tempted toward forms of manipulation that turn Christ's flock into a bleating mass of codependency. The lack of acknowledged power on the part of the pastor is dispersed to the fold and the sheep wander aimlessly in search of some concrete form of guidance. In this instance, the sheep never learn to care for and tend to their own—not to mention others—as their own power has consequently been undermined by the pastor's aversion to power. In both of these cases, the fine balance between power and serving has not been struck and the community, and the good news of the Gospel, suffers.

By contrast, when the Christological vision of the Good Shepherd laying his life down for his sheep is manifest through the offices of power in the church, the church makes visible a form of leadership that uncovers the fears that drive worldly forms of manipulation and replaces them with gestures of trust that come from living truthfully with Christ and one another. Such trust is always tested by our speech. For part of what it means to live truthfully is learning to speak truthfully—and expecting our leaders to do so even when the truth doesn't go down easy. If we resist hearing the truth, our leaders will be tempted to tell us lies and our abiding together becomes farcical.

Truthful speech is at the heart of the matter, for it is through talking to one another that the church discovers what goods we have in common. Those who occupy the ministerial and priestly offices of the church have a particular responsibility for helping the church become articulate, and this is done not through "how-to" lessons but through witness and practice. As our leaders practice an articulate faith in Jesus Christ, through speech and service, we are apprenticed to this peculiar way of speaking and being in the world. Leaders may, from time to time, be those who make "the hard decisions," but more important than the decisions they make is the language that has shaped the decision.

I should like to think such an understanding of leadership is important for helping us understand the work of theology and how that work is central for what seminaries are about. What we teach in seminary is speech. And we learn speech by listening. To return to the parable of the Good Shepherd, in John's Gospel Jesus explains:

> The one who enters the gate is the shepherd of the sheep. The gatekeeper opens the gate for him, and the sheep hear his voice. He calls his own sheep by name and leads them out. When he has brought out all his own, he goes ahead of them,

and the sheep follow him because they know his voice. They will not follow a stranger, but they will run from him because they do not know the voice of strangers. (John 10:2–5)

If the primary task of seminary education is to train pastors as those who will lead the church, then our primary task in seminary education is to train pastors who will recognize the voice of the Good Shepherd so that they may train the rest of the fold to do the same. And we learn the voice of the Good Shepherd by listening and observing how his voice has shaped the hard-won speech of the church through the ages. By tending to the church's speech—how she prays, admonishes, laments, argues—we learn to hear the voice of the Good Shepherd and we learn to test the voice of strangers. Leadership, then, requires both attentive listening and careful speech: wisdom and judgment. If either is avoided the fold, including the pastor, is at risk.

I have been in the business of teaching those called to the ministry for many years. I confess I remain unsure how best to train those going into the ministry, those who will be called upon to be leaders, to be people of wisdom and judgment. How do you train someone to be wise? It is a difficult question that I still seek to answer. But in the very least, those called to occupy the office of theologian for the church must attempt to instill in our students a love of the language of the Gospel, i.e., the voice of the Good Shepherd. For if those called to lead the people of God have confidence and trust in the words we have been given, we can hope that the church will be an alternative to the politics of manipulation that so dominates our world.

20

An Open Letter to Christians Beginning College

The Christian religion is inescapably ritualistic (one is received into the church by a solemn washing with water), uncompromisingly moral ("be ye perfect as your Father in heaven is perfect," said Jesus), and unapologetically intellectual (be ready to give a "reason for the hope that is in you," in the words of 1 Peter). Like all the major religions of the world, Christianity is more than a set of devotional practices and a moral code: It is also a way of thinking about God, about human beings, about the world and history.[1]

Ritualistic, moral, and intellectual: May these words, words that Robert Wilken uses to begin his beautiful book *The Spirit of Early Christian Thought*, be written on your soul as you begin college. Be faithful in worship. In America, going to college is one of those heavily mythologized events that everybody tells you will "change your life," which is probably at least half true. So don't be foolish and imagine that you can take a vacation from church. Uncompromisingly moral? Undergraduate life on college campuses tends in the direction of neo-pagan excess. Good kids from good families too often end up using their four years at college to get drunk and throw

---

1. Robert Wilken, *The Spirit of Early Christian Thought* (New Haven: Yale University Press, 2003), xiii.

up on one another. Too often they do so on their way to the condom dispensers. What a waste.

A waste not only because such behavior is self-destructive, but also because living this way will prevent you from doing the intellectual work that Wilken argues the Christian faith demands. We, that is, the church, need you to do well in school. That may sound strange, because many who represent Christian "values" seem primarily concerned with how you conduct yourself while you are in college. From this perspective, the "Christian part" of being in college is therefore primarily relegated to what is done outside the classroom. What a waste.

The Christian fact is very straightforward: To be a student, to go off to college and spend four years in classes, is a calling. Your parents are setting up accounts to pay the bills, or maybe you are scraping together your own resources and taking out loans, or maybe a big scholarship is making college possible. Whatever the practical source, the end result is the same. You are about to enter a time—four years!—when your main job is to listen to lectures, attend seminars, go to labs, and read books.

What an extraordinary privilege. In a world of deep injustice and violence, a people exist that think some can be given time to study. The metaphysical claims entailed in the theological convictions used to justify the privilege you are being given require your attention. That is particularly true in a time when Christians cannot assume that the world in which we find ourselves has been shaped by Christian presumptions. In such a world, Christians need to be articulate about our faith. If we are not intellectually articulate, we cannot avoid the judgment that what we believe is a matter of opinion. We need you to take seriously the calling that is yours by going to college.

You may well be thinking, "What is he thinking? I am just beginning my freshman year. Why should I think I am being 'called' to be a student? What strange language. None of my peers think they are 'called' to be a student. They just think going to college is a good thing because it 'prepares you for life.' I'm going to college so I can get a better job than those who have not gone to college. Right?"

But you are a Christian. That means you cannot go to college just to get a better job. It's true that these days people talk about college as an "investment," because they think of education like a bank account: You deposit knowledge and expertise, and when it comes time to get a job, you make a withdrawal, putting all that stuff on a resume. Christians need jobs just like anybody else, but the time you spend as an undergraduate is like everything else in your life. It's not "yours" to do with as you please. Christ's call on you as a student is a calling to meet the needs of the church, both for its own life and the life of the world. The resurrection of Jesus, Wilken suggests, is the central fact not only of Christian worship but the ground of all Christian thinking "about God, about human beings, about the world and history." Somebody needs to do that thinking—which means *you*.

Don't underestimate how much the church needs your mind. Remember your study of the Bible? Christians read Isaiah's prophecy of a suffering servant as pointing to Christ. That seems obvious, but it's not, or at least it wasn't obvious to the Ethiopian eunuch to whom the Lord sent Philip to explain things. The church has been explaining, interpreting, and illuminating ever since. Christ is written everywhere, not only in the prophecies of the Old Testament, but on the pages of history and in the book of nature. It takes an educated mind to do the work, the church's work, of proclaiming Christ crucified. And

I don't mean just by way of sermons. I mean by way of thinking about and interpreting the world in light of Christ, often quietly in the solitude of study and sometimes in excited conversations with friends who share your faith. Physics, sociology, French literary theory: all that stuff and more—in fact, everything you study in college—is bathed in the light of Christ. It takes the eyes of faith to see that light, but it also takes an educated mind.

There's a scripture passage that suggests another related dimension of the call to intellectual work. In the first letter of Peter, we read: "Always be ready to make your defense to anyone who demands from you an account of the hope that is in you" (3:15). Not everybody believes. In fact, the contemporary American secular university is largely a place of unbelief. The church, therefore, has a job to do, which is to explain why belief in the power of the risen Lord actually makes sense. There's no one formula, no one argument, so don't imagine that you will find the magic defense against all objections. Anyway, defense isn't the point. Lots of people are lost because they imagine that being a sophisticated contemporary intellectual makes faith impossible. The church wants to reach them, but this requires an ambassador, someone who is at home in the intellectual world. That's you—or at least that's what you can become if you do your work with enthusiasm. Share in a love of learning. It's a worthy love in its own right, and it will allow you to be leaven in the lump of academia.

So, yes, to be a student is a calling, a calling to serve the church and the world. But always remember who serves what. Colleges focus on learning, and in doing so they can create the illusion that being smart and well-educated is the be-all and end-all of life. You do not need to be educated to be a Christian. That's obvious. But you also do not need to be educated to serve the church in many diverse and important ways, some more important than educated analysis and reflection. After all, Christ is most visible to the world in the person who responds to his call: "Come, follow me." I daresay St. Francis of Assisi was more important to the medieval church than any intellectual. One of the most brilliant men in the history of the church, St. Bonaventure, a Franciscan, said as much. But the church needs some Christians to be educated, as St. Bonaventure also knew, which is why he taught at the University of Paris and ensured that, in their enthusiasm for the example of St. Francis, his brother Franciscans didn't give up on education.

The best way to think about the relation between your calling as a student and the many other callings of Christians can be found 1 Corinthians 12. In this letter, Paul is dealing with a community in turmoil. Various factions are claiming priority, a situation that is not hard to imagine today. Teachers think that education is the most important thing. The social activists insist that making the world more just should take priority. Still others insist that internal spiritual renewal is the key to everything. St. Paul, however, reminds the church at Corinth that they are constituted by a variety of gifts that serve to build up the common good of the church. To one is given wisdom, to others knowledge, to still others the work of healing, prophecy, and the discernment of the spirits. So, by all means, honor those who are serving the church in the ordained ministry, or through social action, or through spiritual direction. But remember: You are about to become a student. Whatever you end up doing with your life, now is the time when you will begin to develop the intellectual skills that the church needs for the sake of building up the body of Christ.

Your Christian calling as a student does not require you to become a theologian, at least not in the official sense of the word. Speaking as one whose job title is "professor of theology,"

I certainly hope you will be attracted to the work of theology. These days, at least in the West where the dominant intellectual trends have detached themselves from Christianity, the discipline of theology is in a world of hurt, often tempted by silly efforts to dress up the Gospel in the latest academic fashions. So, God knows, we need all the help we can get. But there is a wider sense of being a theologian, one that simply means thinking about what you are learning in light of Christ. It's possible to be a Christian scholar. This does not happen by making everything fit into church doctrine or biblical preaching—that's theology in the strict, official sense. Instead, to become a Christian scholar is more a matter of intention and desire. The contemporary university is much, much too fragmented to be made into a single system or worldview, and those who try end up creating rickety intellectual contraptions. That's why the church needs you. The witness to Christ in the contemporary world of science, literature, and so forth won't be a grand philosophy; it will be people.

I said people deliberately. You can't do this on your own. You'll need friends who are majoring in physics and biology, as well as economics, psychology, philosophy, literature, and more. They can be fellow students, of course, but many of our intellectual friendships are channeled through books. C. S. Lewis has remained very popular with Christian students for many good reasons, not the least of which is the fact that he makes himself available to his readers as a trusted friend in Christ. That's true for many authors. Get to know them.

Books, moreover, are often the way in which our friendships with our fellow students and teachers begin and are cemented. I'm not a big fan of Francis Schaeffer, but he can be a point of contact, something to agree with or argue about. The same is true for many non-Christian writers who tackle big questions.

Read Plato, not just because you might learn something, but also because reading him will provide a sharpness and depth to your conversations. To a great extent, to be an educated person means having lots of layers to your relationships. Sure, going to the big football game or having a beer (legally) with your buddies should be fun on its own terms, but it's also a reality ripe for analysis, discussion, and conversation. If you read Mary Douglas or Claude Levi-Strauss, then you'll have something to say about the rituals of American sports. And if you read Jane Austen or T.S. Eliot, you will find you are seeing conversations with friends, particularly when sharing a meal, in new ways. And, of course, you cannot read enough Trollope. Think of books, therefore, as the fine thread of a spider's web. They link and connect.

This is especially true for your relationships with your teachers. You are not likely to become buddies with your teachers. They tend to be intimidating. But you can become intellectual friends, and this will most likely happen if you've read some of the same books. This is even true for science professors. You're unlikely to engage a physics professor in an interesting conversation about subatomic particles. As a freshman, you don't know enough. But read C. P. Snow's famous book *Two Cultures*, and I'll bet your physics teacher will want to know what you're thinking. Books are touchstones, common points of reference. They are the water in which our minds swim.

You cannot and should not, therefore, try to avoid being identified as an intellectual. I confess I am not altogether happy with "intellectual" as a description for those who are committed to the work of the university. "Intellectual" is often associated with those who betray a kind of self-indulgence as the result of the assumption that they do not need to justify what they do. It is assumed that "intellectual" work is "important" work.

Knowledge for knowledge's sake is the dogma that is used to justify such an understanding of what it means to be an intellectual. But if you're clear about your calling as a student, then you can avoid that temptation. You are called to the life of the mind in order to be of service to the Gospel and the church. Don't resist this call just because others are misusing it.

Fulfilling your calling as a Christian student won't be easy. It's not easy for anyone who is serious about the intellectual life, Christian or not. Curriculums of many colleges and universities may seem, and in fact may be, chaotic. Many schools have no particular expectations. You check a few general education boxes—a writing course, perhaps, and some general distributional requirements—and then do as you please. Moreover, there is no guarantee that you will be encouraged to read. Some classes, even in the humanities, are based on textbooks that chop up classic texts into little snippets. You cannot become friends with an author by reading half a dozen pages. Finally, and perhaps worse because insidious, there is a strange anti-intellectualism abroad in academia. Some professors have convinced themselves that all knowledge is just political power dressed up in fancy language, or that books and ideas are simply ideological weapons in the quest for domination. Christians, of all people, should recognize that what is known and how it is known produces and reproduces power relations that are unjust, but that does not mean all questions of truth must be abandoned. As I said, it won't be easy.

But you owe it to yourself and the church not to let the incoherence, laziness, and self-critical excesses of the contemporary university demoralize you. Be sure not to let these failures become an excuse for you to avoid an education—a Christian education. Although some universities make it quite easy to avoid being well-educated, I think you will find that every university or college has teachers who deserve the title they've been given. Your task is to find them.

How can you find the best teachers? There are no set principles, but I can suggest guidelines. First, ask around. Are there professors who have reputations as intellectual mentors of Christian students? You're eighteen. You don't need substitute parents. At least, you do not need parents who think you are still twelve, but you do need reliable guides. So rearrange your schedule to take the professor who teaches Dante with sensitivity to the profound theological vision of that great poet. You may end up disagreeing, both with the professor and Dante, but you'll learn how to think as a Christian.

Also, go to the bookstore at the beginning of the term to see which professors assign books—and I mean real books, not textbooks. Textbooks can play a legitimate role in some disciplines, but not all, and never at all levels. You want to find the teachers who have intellectual friends, as it were; teachers who want to share those friends with their students. If a professor has a course outline that gives two or three weeks to reading St. Augustine's *Confessions*, then you can reasonably hope that he thinks of St. Augustine as someone he knows (or wants to know), and someone he wants to share with students.

The best teachers for a Christian student aren't always Christians. In fact, a certain kind of Christian teacher can lead you astray, as it's not easy to see the truth of Christ in modern science or contemporary critical theory, for example. The temptation, therefore, is to compartmentalize, assigning your faith to the heart, perhaps, and then carrying on with your academic work. Some professors have become very comfortable with this compartmentalization. So be careful. By all means take spiritual encouragement wherever you can get it, and these sorts of professors can be helpful in that regard. But don't compartmentalize, because that's basically putting your Christian faith outside of your work as a student. Your calling is to be a Christian student. The Christian part and the student part are inseparable. It will be hard and frustrating, because you won't see how they go together. Nobody does, at least not in the complete sense of having worked it all out. But you need to remember that Christ said, "I am the Alpha and the Omega." However uncertain we are about the *how*, we know *that* Christian goes with student (and teacher).

Although many professors are not Christians, and at some schools most aren't, many have a piety that is especially relevant to the academic life. One, for example, might be committed to the intrinsic importance of knowing Wordsworth's poetry, or another to getting the chemistry experiment right. These professors convey a spirit of devotion. Their intellectual lives serve the subject matter rather than treating it as information to be mastered, or worse, as a dead body of knowledge that must be conveyed to students. English literature and modern science do not exist for their own sakes, and the university doesn't raise money for the sake of their careers. For these professors, then, the educational system exists for the sake of their disciplines, which they willingly serve. This spirit of devotion is not the same as Christian faith, but it can help shape your young intellectual desires and impulses in the right way, reminding you that your job as a student is to serve and not to be served. College isn't for you; it's for your Christian calling as an intellectual.

Eventually you will no longer be a freshman, and American undergraduate education will force you to begin to specialize. There are dangers as well as opportunities. You will be tempted to choose a major that will give you a sense of coherence. But be careful that your major does not narrow you in the wrong way. It's true, for example, that modern psychology provides powerful insights into the human condition, but don't allow your increasing expertise to lure you into illusions of mastery. Continue reading broadly. It may seem that the more you know about less and less, the smarter you've become. After all, you now know so much more about psychology. But in truth, the more you know about less and less should teach you humility. After a couple of years taking advanced courses in modern European history, you'll know more about the French Revolution, but if you're self-reflective, you'll also know how much work it takes to know anything well. And there's so much more to know about reality than modern European history.

In order to combat a tendency toward the complacency that comes from mastering a discipline, it is particularly important that you gain historical insight as to why your discipline is practiced the way it currently is. For example, I have nothing but high regard for the disciplines we group under the somewhat misleading category "the sciences," but too often students have no idea how and why the scientific fields' research agendas developed in the forms in which they are now practiced. Reading Isaac Newton can be a bit of a shock, because he interwove his scientific analysis with theological arguments. You shouldn't take that as a mandate for doing the same thing in the twenty-first century, but it should make you realize that modern science has profound metaphysical and theological dimensions that have been cordoned off, perhaps for good reasons. Or perhaps not. The point is that knowing the history of your discipline will inevitably broaden the kinds of questions you ask, forcing you to read in order to be an intellectual rather than just a specialist.

It is important, moreover, that you not accept as a given the categorizations that dominate the contemporary university. For example, if you read Dante you will probably do so in the English department. The English department has claimed Dante because they claim that the *Inferno* is "literature." Dante was obviously a poet, and one of the most influential, but he was also a theologian, and we fail to do him justice if we ignore the fact that quite specific theological convictions, some controversial in his own day and ours as well, were at the center of his life and work. The same can be said for theology, which often imagines that a particular form of scholastic and philosophically-shaped reflection defines the discipline, while ignoring the mystical traditions, as well as the traditions of biblical commentary.

I emphasize broadening your major with historical questions and challenges to set categories because your calling is to be a Christian student, not a physics student or an English student. Again, I do not want to make every Christian in the university into a theologian, but it is very important for you to interrogate theologically what you are learning. For example, you may major in economics—a discipline currently dominated by mathematical models and rational choice theories. Those theories may have some utility, to use an economic expression, but they may also entail anthropological assumptions that a Christian cannot accept. You will not be in a position to even see the problem, much less address it, if you let your intellectual life be defined by your discipline.

There's more to say, and I wish I could give more practical, concrete advice. But most of academic life is, as Tip O'Neill said of politics, "local." Theology programs at some nominally Christian colleges are positively harmful to the calling of the Christian student; others are wonderfully helpful. For some students, a professor who avows atheism may be their first encounter with a teacher who thinks faith is relevant to the intellectual life, albeit in a purely negative way. The encounter need not harm the Christian student. It might galvanize convictions and set the student on the course of figuring out how faith supports and motivates the intellectual life. Nonetheless, as I have tried to emphasize, you need good mentors, men and women who are dedicated to their work, and for whom a fitting humility about the limits of their expertise lead them to read broadly and thus become intellectuals rather than specialists.

I want to end by returning to Robert Wilken's observation about the ritual, moral, and intellectual life of the Christian. Don't fool yourself. Only a man or a woman who has undergone a long period of spiritual discipline can reliably pray in the solitude of a hermitage. You're young. You need the regular discipline of worship, Bible reading, and Christian fellowship. Don't neglect them in college. Also, don't underestimate the moral temptations of the contemporary college scene. We cannot help but be influenced by the behavior of our friends, so choose wisely.

To worship God and live faithfully are necessary conditions if you are to survive in college. But as a Christian you are called to do more than survive. As a Christian, you are called to use the opportunity you have been given to learn to construe the world as a creature of a God who would have us enjoy and bask in the love that has brought us into existence. God has given your mind good work to do. As a member of the church, we're counting on you. It won't be easy. It never has been. But I can testify that it can also be a source of joy.

What a wonderful adventure you have before you. I wish you well.

21

Sexing the Ministry

I often observe that it is not the ordination of gays that threatens the ministry. Rather, the biggest problem is adultery. I then observe that I wish that adultery could be attributed to lust, but most people in ministry do not have that much energy. Rather, I attribute much of the adultery committed by those in the ministry to loneliness. For I take it that in the ministry, loneliness surrounds those who occupy the office of priest or minister.

I think it is important to ask why that is the case. I suspect it has to do with the lack of understanding by those the minister serves of what the ministry entails. Many operate under the presumption that those in the ministry are only required to work one day a week. Beyond this single day of work, what is required of those in the ministry is that they be personable. At the very least, this means they are to be superficially friendly with everyone in the congregation. If the minister becomes a genuine friend with some members in their congregation, it may seem the minister is playing favorites and, therefore, cannot deliver pastoral services in a fair manner to everyone in the congregation.

Pastoral services, moreover, can be one of the sources of the profound loneliness associated with the ministry. Priests and ministers are often given permission to be present to people in some of the most agonizing events in life. Divorce, death, and destruction name some events in which ministers are asked to participate in order to provide comfort. During the crisis, the family or other members of the church are glad the priest is there to pray for them. But too often, after the crisis has passed, those who have gone through it do not want anything to do with the minister because the minister has witnessed them in their most vulnerable moments. Having been naked with emotion, they fear those with such knowledge. The minister is, so to speak, stiff-armed. The intensity of the events into which they were invited cannot be shared, given the obligations regarding confidentiality associated with such privilege. This makes the priest even more isolated from those he or she serves.

All this is complicated by the politics of ministerial placement. It is hard to be friends with others in your own denomination because you may be in competition with them. Friendship is possible with other clergy, but perhaps most easily when they serve in another denomination. Moreover, such friendships too often consist of sharing war stories about how bad the congregations you serve may be. Friendships based on such dismal data are not likely to last.

It is true, moreover, that those in the congregation often assume they can place infinite demands on their minister. It does not take long, therefore, for those in the ministry to feel as if they have been nibbled to death by ducks. Some priests try to escape through the route of clinical pastoral education. Others retreat into their family because those duties and obligations are easy to explain. But this creates its own problems because no spouse is required to love another spouse that much. Spouses may be friends but it is not a condition necessary to make a marriage a marriage.

I realize that this characterization of how the ministry can result in making priests and ministers feel alone may be far too dour a view, but I suspect most in the ministry will detect some truth to the picture I have painted. I think, moreover, that what I have described helps us understand how those in the ministry often find themselves in compromised sexual circumstances. Clergy are often desperate to be known by another human being. It is not accidental that sexual relations are often described in the Bible as a "knowing."

For example, one of the tasks that often falls on those in the ministry is to counsel people whose marriages are in trouble. Counseling itself can a produce a form of (false) intimacy. It is easy to imagine, given the loneliness I have suggested is characteristic of the ministry, finding yourself attracted to the person you are counseling. Too often, the touch of the hand to comfort someone who has broken into tears can lead to touching that had not been planned. Before you know it, you have been pulled into a "spontaneous" relationship you had not anticipated—a relationship thought to be all the more significant exactly because it "just happened." Some may well think this is a far too innocent account of sexual misconduct by those in the ministry. I am sure that sexual misconduct has multiple sources. I am also sure that the ministry attracts out-and-out sexual predators. It is often said that such people, like rapists, are not really attracted to sex. They are really attracted to power over others. Given the powerlessness that those in the ministry often feel, one can see how the exercise of power through sex may be a form of compensation. But I have never been convinced it really is a matter of power. It really is a matter of sex. That it really is a matter of sex, moreover, is a reminder that sex, whether between strangers or those who have been long married, can be and is often a very violent physical act.

I do not want to be misunderstood. I am not suggesting that ministerial misconduct in matters sexual is not an abuse of power.

I have no doubt that just as a teacher is not to be involved with a student, those in the ministry abuse the power they have been given if they become involved sexually with one of the members of their congregation. What I am objecting to, however, is the presumption that what is wrong with that kind of ministerial misconduct can be captured solely by the description "the abuse of power." That the abuse of power takes the form of sexual misconduct is not irrelevant for how we should think about these matters. I suspect the temptation to describe such misconduct as an abuse of power suggests part of the problem is that the church no longer knows what it wants or needs to say about sex. As a result, those in the ministry, as well as those they serve, are left with little guidance about how we should conduct ourselves sexually.

We are unsure where even to begin to think morally about sex. What I am sure of is that we will not have a sufficient ethic about the sexual behavior of those in the ministry by focusing on sex itself. Indeed, I do not believe any sexual ethic is possible by focusing on sex alone. Rather, how you think about what is appropriate or inappropriate sexual behavior will, by necessity, draw on more determinative ways of life than sexuality. That I have diagnosed one of the reasons for sexual misconduct as a response to the loneliness of the lives of those in the ministry reflects my presumption that the sexual character of our lives must be surrounded by richer forms of life than sex itself. For example, if the church is a community committed to speaking the truth to one another, that should make a difference for how we relate sexually. To engage in sex outside of marriage involves secrecy. And secrecy is the breeding ground of the lie. Accordingly, it becomes extremely important to see the connections between significant practices that must be interrelated if we are to live with integrity.

Indeed I suspect the overdetermination of the importance of sex in our society has everything to do with the loss of other significant forms of human relatedness. For example, ask yourself why people in significant friendships think it important *not* to be involved sexually with one another. Sex is a far too complicated form of life to be introduced into the relation between friends. When friends become sexually involved, you can be sure that something other than friendship has begun.

In truth, contrary to what we often tell the young, you do not need to know another person to have what might be considered "good sex." It is often forgotten that Christians assumed for centuries that a couple who had not known one another until the day of the marriage would have sex after they have been declared married not because they "loved" or even knew one another but because they were married. They might come to love one another by being married and that love might involve their sexual behavior, but what made their sexual relations legitimate was the reality that they could be held responsible for any children that resulted from their sexual relation. In other words, marriage meant they were having sex "in public."

In the absence of significant relationships that should surround how sex might contribute to a life lived with purpose, I fear that we now live in a society in which sex is used as entertainment or as a desperate way to overwhelm our loneliness. It is not only those in the ministry who live lives of loneliness. In truth, all our lives are gripped by a profound sense of loneliness. Sports fans may enjoy being a part of the crowd at games or bars as this kind of belonging temporarily combats the loneliness we all desire to overcome. Sex, like the crowd, too often becomes an ultimately unsatisfying way to connect with another human being with whom we share the shallowest of interests.

Pornography is the ultimate attempt to make sex in itself self-fulfilling. The result, interestingly enough, is boredom.

I assume that Christians, including those in the ministry, are no less determined by the way sex is construed in our culture than those who are not Christian. Sex has become the last sacrament, that is, it is assumed some meaning or reality will result from sexual behavior no matter what intentions you bring to the act. This has become particularly destructive for young people who now engage in sexual relations with one another in a manner that makes sex a far too manipulative reality in their lives. Why, for example, do we not call the intercourse had when the seventeen-year-old left tackle of the football team convinces the unattractive thirteen-year-old to engage in it, "rape"?

To tell young people that sex is such a precious form of relating that they should save it for when they are "really in love" is a formula for disaster. The result is that kids who should not be in love, whatever it might mean to be in love, think they are in love because they are having sex. They are having sex, moreover, because sex turns out to be more interesting than anything else in their lives. It is the way they try to understand what adult relations may entail. The result is the development of a perspective on sex that makes it just another form of "relating." It is, of course, another form of relating, but it is one fraught with bodily implications that most people are ill-prepared to negotiate. Just to take off one's clothes, to become naked, in the presence of another creates an intimacy that is often unanticipated.

I mention these general attitudes and behaviors surrounding sex in the world because our inability to have a language to talk about sex in church is an indication of the loneliness I am suggesting shapes our lives. One of the difficulties ministers face when it comes to sex in their lives, as well as the lives of those they serve, is we seem to have lost the ability to talk about sex in a manner that is not deceptive. One of the reasons for our inability to talk to one another about sex, as I suggested above, is the loss of any determinative behavior that gives purpose to our lives when it comes to sex. In other words, we cannot develop an adequate account of the role of sex in our lives by focusing on sexual acts or something called "our sexuality" that allegedly always needs to be expressed. Rather we can only get a handle on sex by identifying those forms of life that give purpose to our sexual behavior. For that to take place means we must be able to have an adequate way to talk to one another about our lives sexually that preserves the intimacy that rightly surrounds sexual expression by those committed to keeping faith with one another.

For that to happen, I think, will require the church to discover determinative practices—practices, as I suggested above, as basic as speaking the truth to one another—some of which may seem quite odd. For example, I think what must be said about sex by Christians is that sex is not all it is cracked up to be. You are not less a human being, and you are certainly not less a Christian, if you have never had a sexual relation with another human being. Remember that one of the most significant developments in the early church was the presumption that if you were a Christian you did not have to marry or have children. I do not think that presumption was the result of Christian disdain for sexual activity, but rather it was an expression of the Christian commitment to grow the church through witness and conversion rather than biology. Of course Christians could marry, but those who married, interestingly, bore the burden of proof, given that they did not need to do so to be a Christian. For what the single gave up was not sex, though they were certainly expected to live exemplary lives, but heirs. Those called to marriage understood their calling might well entail the willingness to welcome new life. For, if I am right that those called to marriage in the Christian community bear the burden of proof, one of the questions they must ask is whether they are willing to receive those who may come from, be born of, this marriage. Marriage is not the end in itself, but rather an institution of hope in a world of despair. I am not suggesting that every act of sexual intercourse must be open to procreation, but rather that marriage as a practice is unintelligible if the role of children is not constitutive of what marriage is about.

A community so determined must be one in which those who constitute it have the gift of friendship. For singleness cannot be sustained without friendship. (Neither, of course, can marriage or parenting.) But the friendship made possible by being Christian is the result of having good work to share. In other words, friendship is not an end in itself, but rather comes from the discovery that we need one another, given the task of being God's people in a world that knows not the God of Jesus Christ. When the ministry is threatened by sexual misconduct, we have an indication that the church has lost sight of the work we have been given to do, that is, of our purpose.

Friendship requires the ability of friends (whether married or single) to be able to talk to one another about what they fear. What most of us fear is that we cannot be loved. Sex often becomes a way to assure ourselves that we are capable of being loved. But that turns out to be a doubtful strategy for the long run because it results in manipulative behavior that is hard to recognize exactly because the behavior is thought to be an expression of love. Priests, as well as their congregants, discover they are being held captive to accounts of sex they often recognize as destructive but have no way to free themselves from those accounts because they have lost the ability to speak honestly about their lives.

So I think if we want to make a start to help those in the ministry have an adequate sexual ethic, we must begin by asking them to think twice about the language we use about sex. For example, it is not a bad place to start to call into question the very notions of "sexual ethics," "professional ethics," or "professional sexual ethics." Those phrases suggest that professional sexual ethics can be isolated from other aspects of our lives in such a way as only to reinforce the problems we are confronting in the first place. To try to develop a sexual ethic divorced from the traditional Christian position that some are called to the life of singleness (a life that may entail vowed celibacy) while others are called to marriage cannot avoid misconstruing the crucial theological moves entailed in serious discernment about these matters.

To develop a sexual ethic on the basis of what makes sex good will never work because sex is a far too complex form of behavior to be "controlled" by isolating it. To try to address sexual ethics as an end in itself is about as silly as telling someone obsessed by sex to try not to think about sex. The very attempt not to think about sex means you cannot help but think about sex most of the time. The only way to help someone obsessed by sex is to give them some good work to do, that is, work that is so demanding that they discover new habits that shape their imaginations. Of course, it is not just their imaginations that are so shaped, but it is their bodies.

I suspect, for example, that one of the most important developments to free women from the male gaze has been the involvement of women in sports and in the professions. Women have been given good work to do that challenges the male presumption that women are primarily to be regarded in terms of their sexual attractiveness. I am not suggesting that athletic women are not attractive, but rather women athletes present an alternative image that contradicts the all-too-prevalent images of female seduction in our society.

The analysis I have given and the constructive alternative I have tried to provide may seem not to have addressed issues surrounding ministerial sexual misconduct. In my defense, I have tried to reframe how we should think about ministerial sexual ethics. By directing attention to our societal confusions about sex as well as the reproduction of those confusions in the church itself, I have tried to suggest why we have failed to understand how and why sexual misconduct is such a threat to the ministry. The loneliness of the minister is only made more destructive by the inability of the church to have a language that makes possible communication between people about our sexual lives. We need to be able to talk frankly with one another about sex, but that requires trust.

The development of such trust surely depends on the acknowledgment that whatever sexual history we may bring to such discussions it is not determinative for what we as Christians think we now need to say. What I suspect destroys many is not what they have done sexually but the justifications they have given for what they have done. Too often those justifications turn out to be exercises in self-deception that mire us deeper in ways of life that force us into secrecy. As a result we end up becoming strangers to ourselves and strangers to those with whom we worship.

There is no quick fix for the fix we find ourselves in when it comes to sex and, in particular, how the ministry has been sexed. I do not think this is necessarily bad news. But it does require

Christians to resist the myths that surround sex in our society. Such a resistance will require people who are determined to speak truthfully to one another about the confusions that constitute our lives when it comes to sex. Such people I would hope might include those called "Reverend" or "Pastor." In short, they are people who lead lives that make it possible for them to tell us the truth. So understood, they are people who have good but difficult work to do. But what a blessing that must be in a time when so many now think there is no good work to be done.